FAITHFUL LIVING
in a
FAITHLESS WORLD

ROY CLEMENTS

InterVarsity Press
Downers Grove, Illinois

InterVarsity Press
P.O. Box 1400, Downers Grove, IL 60515
World Wide Web: www.ivpress.com
E-mail: mail@ivpress.com

InterVarsity Press®is the book-publishing division of InterVarsity Christian Fellowship®, a student movement active on campus at hundreds of universities, colleges and schools of nursing in the United States of America, and a member movement of the International Fellowship of Evangelical Students. For information about local and regional activities, write Public Relations Dept., InterVarsity Christian Fellowship, 6400 Schroeder Rd., P.O. Box 7895, Madison, WI 53707-7895.

Cover photograph: SuperStock

ISBN 0-8308-1945-2

Printed in the United States of America ♾

Library of Congress Cataloging-in-Publication Data

Clements, Roy.
  [Practising faith in a pagan world]
  Faithful living in a faithless world / Roy Clements.
    p. cm.
  Originally published: Practising faith in a pagan world. England.
1997.
    ISBN 0-8308-1945-2 (pbk.: alk. paper)
    1. Bible.   O.T. Ezekiel—Sermons.   2. Bible.   O.T. Daniel—
Sermons.   3. Baptists—Sermons.   4. Sermons, English.   I. Title.
    BS1545.4.C54   1998
224'.406—dc21   98-18561
                                                                        CIP

20	19	18	17	16	15	14	13	12	11	10	9	8	7	6	5	4	3	2	1
15	14	13	12	11	10	09	08	07	06	05	04	03	02	01	00	99	98

Preface

The chapters that follow began as two series of sermons delivered at Eden Baptist Church in Cambridge, England. They were adapted later into a single series of expositions and delivered as autumn lectures for the Proclamation Trust at St. Helens, Bishopsgate, London, in 1990.

In adapting them once again, I owe a debt of thanks to Inter-Varsity Press of the United Kingdom, and particularly to Marie Palmer, who transcribed the tape recordings of the lectures, and Jo Bramwell, who edited them for publication. The addresses were not intended for that purpose, and the acute reader will detect some overlap of content within the chapters. Those familiar with other published sermons of mine will observe some additional duplication of material. This, I fear, is an occupational hazard to which all preachers are vulnerable. By far the larger part of what follows, however, has not been reproduced anywhere else, and, although it is some years now since it was first presented, I believe that its central theme is still immensely relevant.

I often find myself rather uncomfortably in a minority these days at conferences of evangelical Christians. Most of my fellow believers are singing triumphalist choruses about imminent revival. Some even offer prophetic words assuring us that God is about to do something absolutely tremendous in our culture. But like the little boy in the famous story of the emperor's new clothes, I simply do not see it. Perhaps I am blind through lack of faith. Readers must judge for themselves. What I do see in the Western world at the end of the twentieth century is a relentless slide back into pagan superstition. Not only has Christianity been reduced to the status of a minority cult, but postmodern skepticism now casts doubt on science, reason and the very existence of an accessible, objective truth, external to the human mind.

Of course, a massive revival of biblical Christianity is possible in such a society. But it would involve a miracle on a scale far larger than that experienced in any revival history has so far produced. We live no longer in Jerusalem but in Athens. The current popularity of talk about spirituality must not seduce us into unwarranted optimism. Not every spirit is the Spirit of God (see 1 Jn 4:1-3). Revival requires that men and women go beyond the mere quest for spiritual self-fulfillment and psychic awareness and have dealings with a personal God about their sins. In this respect the aspirations of New Age mysticism are as far from authentic Christianity as was the atheistic humanism that preceded it.

No, I do not believe we are standing with Peter on the threshold of a new Pentecost, anticipating the imminent conversion of thousands daily. We are sharing, rather, with Ezekiel and Daniel in a new Babylonian exile. If we learn the lessons these two great men of God can teach us, our valley of dry bones may yet see resurrection. But it is not as imminent, nor will it be as pain-free, as those triumphalist choruses of ours make out.

Introduction

Not so long ago most people in the West would have called themselves Christians. Other religions existed, of course, but they were so remote from our culture and location that they could be disdained as mere pagan superstitions. There were skeptical philosophers, some of whom even dared to confess themselves openly as atheists, but such opinions were generally regarded as bizarre and even scandalous. Toleration in the eighteenth and nineteenth centuries in Britain referred only to different branches of the church. No one seriously suggested that those of other faiths, or even of no faith at all, should be treated with the same respect as a Christian gentleman. The very idea was unthinkable. Christendom was synonymous in the Western mind with civilization. Those who did not subscribe to the former had very dubious title to the latter.

One does not have to be an acute social observer to realize that the past century has witnessed an extraordinary reversal of that Christian privilege. Under the pressure of international trade, technological advances in transportation and communication and, perhaps most serious of all, the fear of war, we can no longer treat other religions with indifference. The world has become a global village, and other religions are now on our doorstep. Indeed, migration has brought mosques and temples to the main streets of Western nations. Nor can irreligion any longer be dismissed as an eccentricity espoused only by a lunatic fringe. Any religious education teacher in Britain will confirm that in an average class of schoolchildren today, you will not find more than one or two who are willing to be known by their peers as Christians.

The Christian consensus—for over a millennium the ideological foundation of European civilization—is crumbling away. In its place a new kind of society is emerging. There are still plenty of church spires on the city skyline, but they are dwarfed by the skyscrapers of contemporary commerce. Bishops still sit in the House of Lords, but their influence in the political direction of Britain today is almost nil. The monarch is still crowned in Westminster Abbey, but it may only be a matter of time before that ceremony is either abolished or turned into a multifaith service. Pluralism has been effectively accepted as the new social reality, and Christianity is increasingly marginalized, privatized and neutralized.

Statistical analysis over the last twenty years has shown quite clearly that numbers of church members in the United Kingdom have been declining constantly over that period. If that trend is not arrested, by the year 2070 there will be no church members at all.

The trend is being arrested, however. There is an underlying groundswell, and that is a cause of encouragement. Some Christians are responding to the bleak picture of the decline of Christian influence in the West by predicting very confidently that we are on the threshold of a major revival. Some even undertake ambitious prayer marches to claim back territory for Jesus from the demonic principalities and powers that have usurped the land.

No one would be more overjoyed than I if this optimism proved to be justified. But there is another possible scenario, one for which the books of Ezekiel and Daniel are uniquely placed to prepare the church. In the days of those prophets as well there was popular talk of speedy restoration and revival. But that was not the message God had actually given them. The prophets were very much in the minority, speaking rather of a tragic time of exile for the people of God. For this less happy prospect the Western church also must be prepared.

One

Called to Be God's Watchman

EZEKIEL 1—3

*T*he period of Ezekiel and Daniel found the Jewish community in a world uncannily like our own in some respects: a world of intoxicating economic affluence and intimidating power politics, but no longer shaped by the biblical values and ideas that had been foundational to Jewish culture. The first two verses of the book of Daniel describe the historical background.

> In the third year of the reign of Jehoiakim king of Judah, Nebuchadnezzar king of Babylon came to Jerusalem and besieged it. And the Lord delivered Jehoiakim king of Judah into his hand, along with some of the articles from the temple of God. These he carried off to the temple of his god in Babylonia and put in the treasure house of his god. (1:1-2)

The story, then, is set in the exile, when the cream of Jewish society was skimmed out of Jerusalem and deported to the vast metropolis of Nebuchadnezzar's Babylon. It was a beautiful city, renowned in the ancient world, at that time in process of reconstruction but soon to become one of the wonders of the ancient world. It was a city more impressive, more advanced in architecture and technology, than anything the Jews had ever seen before. It was a magnificent city that made even Jerusalem at its height, in the days of Solomon, look dull and primitive by comparison. Most of all it was a victorious city, the capital of an empire that had humiliated the armies of the ancient world, including Judah.

The tragedy would probably not have been quite so serious if the Jews had been prepared to accept this situation with good grace, pay their taxes to Babylon and keep a low profile. But an insane, triumphalist, national pride refused to let them do that. In 598 B.C. their king, Jehoiakim, rebelled. Babylonian reprisals were swift and effective; the rebellion was crushed. Jehoiakim was captured, probably in battle, and died shortly afterwards, possibly assassinated by his own people in order to secure a more merciful settlement. The city of Jerusalem surrendered after a brief siege. Jehoiakim's son Jehoiachin, who had been on the throne only three months, together with ten thousand members of the Jewish aristocracy and the intellectual elite, were transported across the desert to Babylonia.

It was a shattering blow. Imagine, for one awful moment, that an enemy power had conquered your country, captured you and forcibly transported you to a permanent new location in some foreign place. Even for those of us who are used to traveling abroad, it would be a humiliating experience. It was even more traumatic for the Jews, because not only had the vast majority of them never visited a foreign country before, but their whole national ideology centered around that tiny principality of Judah and its capital city, Jerusalem. This was the land of Canaan, the divine bequest to Abraham and his descendants forever. This was the throne city of David, the royal dynasty that could never cease. This was the temple of Yahweh, the invincible God, before whom all other gods were supposed to be powerless idols. To be a Jew and to be cut off from these sacred things was to jeopardize not just their cultural identity but their very faith itself. That which for centuries they thought utterly impossible had happened. They had lost the promised land. They were exiles.

Some could not absorb the shock. Mournfully they sat in their riverside encampments bemoaning the loss of their homeland: "By the rivers of Babylon we sat and wept when we remembered Zion. . . . How can we sing the songs of the LORD while in a foreign land?" (Ps 137:1, 4).

Others found that bitterness and resentment against their Babylonian masters fed the fires of their old political defiance once again. They refused to believe that what had happened was anything more than a temporary hiccup. There were plenty of Jews left. Jerusalem under Zedekiah, Jehoiachin's uncle, was still a viable proposition. They were not finished yet! The situation was going to turn around; there would soon be a great restoration. These Chaldean imperialists would get what was coming to them: "O Daughter of Babylon, doomed to destruction, happy is he who repays you for what you have done to us" (Ps 137:8).

Such hopes of speedy restoration, however, proved illusory. The seizure of tribute from the temple was only the beginning. Twenty years after the first subjugation of the Jews, Nebuchadnezzar's troops had to return to Jerusalem to suppress rebellion, and on the final visit, around 587 B.C., the emperor's patience came to an end. He razed the city and its temple to the ground, and exiled not just a handful of aristocrats to Babylon, but the bulk of the entire Jewish population.

Like us, these Jews were hovering between hope and despair. Some were saying that revival was just around the corner; others were saying that it was not. Like us, they could remember when biblical religion dominated their social horizons, but now paganism was no longer remote. They could no longer despise it as an inferior superstition, for they no longer lived in a theocratic state where religion and politics were so entangled that it was impossible to separate them. The days when, to be anything in society, you had to be a faithful Jew, were gone for good.

The world had shrunk. These rivals to biblical religion were not only on the doorstep; they had crossed the threshold, and the Jews found themselves stripped of all their former privileges and power in a vast secular empire. It was no longer to anybody's advantage to be a practicing Jew. On the contrary, social advancement was much more likely to come to those who showed themselves willing to adjust to the culture and lifestyle of their imperial masters.

The challenge then was very similar to that which faces Christians today. How do we understand what has happened to the church? How do we interpret this decline of biblical religion in Protestant countries? Is it a temporary hiccup? Is it just a lull between two great revivals? Or is it more serious than that? How can we sustain and practice biblical faith in a secular society in which Christians are reduced to an unfashionable and odd minority?

The books of Ezekiel and Daniel are uniquely placed to answer such questions. The exile, to which they relate, tells us something about a church in decline, a church which no longer has power, and a Christian population that feels itself to be a minority, maybe an increasingly disadvantaged minority.

Both Ezekiel and Daniel divide into two sections. Ezekiel 1—24 deals with the early part of the exile; in it the prophet is interpreting theologically the reasons for the disgrace of Israel and the triumph of paganism. Daniel's first part, chapters 1—6, comprises stories designed to strengthen the faith of pious Jews in exile, and to help them adapt to being without the support of a national culture for their faith. In their closing chapters both books point to the future, to the authentic hope that the true prophets held out to the people of God in those dreary days of exile. This hope of the kingdom of God, unlike the monarchy of Israel or the great pagan emperors of Babylon and its successors, would last forever.

God's Prophet Introduced

The book of Ezekiel is not easy. Most people who try to study it give up within a few chapters. There are a number of reasons for that. For a start, Ezekiel's writing is often ponderous and repetitive. In addition, the bulk of the book is obsessed with divine retribution, an unpleasant subject at the best of times, and made far more unpalatable by the bloodcurdling ferocity of some of Ezekiel's language.

But perhaps the most difficult thing about the book is the character of Ezekiel himself. In the whole of the Bible, there nowhere appears a more extraordinary figure. There is his habit, for instance, of illustrating his sermons with bizarre antics. Those who are interested in illustrating gospel preaching with drama must find a great advocate in Ezekiel, especially in chapters 4—7. He cuts off his beard with a sword, weighs it, cuts it up, burns it, throws it in the air and finally sews it into the hem of his coat. He digs a tunnel out of his own house rather than use the front door. He lies on his side for a whole year, eating food cooked over cow dung.

On top of this there are his apparent psychic powers: his telepathy that permits him to see in detail events taking place five hundred miles away, and his ability to levitate, which enables him on occasion to rise above the surface of the earth and even to travel over it at remarkable speed. There are his outlandish visual experiences. There is his unnatural composure in the face of his wife's sudden death. There is the strange inability to speak that seems to have afflicted him on and off throughout his ministry. In short, just about everything about this man looks abnormal.

He was probably a priest's son; that seems to be the implication of the phrase "Ezekiel the priest, the son of Buzi" (1:3). Presumably he was therefore a member of the tribe of Levi. He was certainly one of the ten thousand elite who had been deported with Jehoiachin, meaning that as well as being a priest, he was a man of high rank in society. We find him sitting later among the elders of Israel, apparently commanding considerable respect.

But in spite of his aristocratic connections, Ezekiel was not by training a politician or landowner. His priesthood may be the clue to understanding the early example of eccentricity that bursts upon us in the opening chapter. Quite suddenly and without warning, we are told that the heavens opened and Ezekiel saw visions of God (1:1). According to the Levitical law, priests began their public ministry at the age of thirty, and that might be why Ezekiel begins this chapter with "In the thirtieth year." Verse 2 makes it plain that the year in question was the fifth year of Jehoiachin's exile, 593 B.C., which as far as we know was not the thirtieth year of anything special. It was probably the age of Ezekiel at this time.

Perhaps we should imagine this young man wandering beside the part of the river to which his group of exiles had been sent, thinking about his future. This was his thirtieth year, maybe even his thirtieth birthday. If he had been back in Jerusalem, this would have been a time of celebration, for he would have been committing his life to the divine vocation of service in the temple. No doubt his father Buzi had taught him to look forward to that ever since he was a child. As a priest he would have the privilege of touching holy things, maybe even of entering the sanctuary itself one day as high priest and seeing Yahweh's throne. Of all the Jews, it must have been the priests who felt the severance from Jerusalem the most intensely.

Instead, they were removed far from the ark of the covenant, surrounded as it was by cherubim, full of smoke and fire, the symbol of God's living presence in the midst of his people, just as the book of Moses had described. Such thoughts must have been implanted deep in the young Ezekiel's mind by his father. But now such juvenile ambitions were nothing but empty dreams. The exiles were five hundred miles from Jerusalem, and who could tell what would become of the temple? There were rumors that Zedekiah was going to rebel again, given the opportunity. What would happen if he did? Would God miraculously

intervene and save Jerusalem, as he had done in the days of
Hezekiah when the Assyrians attacked the city? Some prophets
said that he undoubtedly would. Within a few months we'll all
be back in our homes, they proclaimed, and everything will be
back to normal. Don't worry, God is on our side. He's going to
do something great, and soon.

Were they right? Indeed, was God's arm long enough to
stretch those five hundred miles from Jerusalem to the River
Kebar in Babylonia? Even if it was, would he be willing to stretch
it out to deliver his people at this time?

Perhaps this young man was a little depressed, a little disappointed, certainly disturbed and bewildered, as he strolled aim-
lessly along the bank of the river. We can picture him so deep in
thought that he does not notice the approaching desert storm
until it is almost upon him. Suddenly he is plunged into a furious
cauldron of thunder and lightning. As the natural elements do
their best to terrify him, he finds himself face to face with
something utterly supernatural. Did I say "something"? No,
someone!

God's Presence Revealed

Spread out above the heads of the living creatures was what
looked like an expanse, sparkling like ice and awesome. Under the expanse their wings were stretched out one toward the
other, and each had two wings covering its body. When the
creatures moved, I heard the sound of their wings, like the
roar of rushing waters, like the voice of the Almighty, like the
tumult of an army. When they stood still they lowered their
wings.

Then there came a voice from above the expanse over their
heads as they stood with lowered wings. Above the expanse
over their heads was what looked like a throne of sapphire,
and high above on the throne was a figure like that of a man.
I saw that from what appeared to be his waist up he looked

like glowing metal, as if full of fire, and that from there down
he looked like fire; and brilliant light surrounded him. Like
the appearance of a rainbow in the clouds on a rainy day, so
was the radiance around him.

This was the appearance of the likeness of the glory of the
Lord. When I saw it, I fell facedown. (1:22-28)

Skeptics have not been slow to interpret such experiences as
hallucinations, or to diagnose Ezekiel as a paranoid schizophrenic. Science fiction addicts have seized upon this event as
an early encounter with a flying saucer. If we had no other data
to go on, we might devise some such explanation ourselves. But
a comparison with the experience of other prophets makes such
speculations unnecessary. Ezekiel's experience here was unusual, but not unique. It was clearly a theophany, a direct visual
revelation of God such as some of the other prophets had
received, such as Moses on Sinai (Ex 33:12—34:8) or Isaiah in
the temple (Is 6).

We should not get too bogged down with the detail of the
prophet's portrayal of this vision. Notice the repetition of words
such as *appearance* and *likeness*. When he summons enough courage to speak of the representation of God that he sees, he piles
qualification upon qualification to make sure that nobody could
think he is actually telling us what God looks like. "This was the
appearance of the likeness of the glory of the Lord," he says,
putting three words between what he saw and what the Lord is
really like. Ezekiel is conscious that he is trying to describe the
indescribable. His language may well be symbolic, chosen to
communicate the emotional shock of what he saw, or its theological significance, rather than an attempt to reproduce in our
imaginations an exact picture of what it was he felt and saw. In
terms of literary art, this is an impressionistic account.

Ezekiel is contributing to the development of *apocalyptic*, a
literary genre that is not intended to be understood literally. The
way to read Ezekiel's account is to try to distill its overall emo-

tional impact out of its coded symbolism. It then becomes clear that what Ezekiel saw was God's throne, something very similar to the man-made representation of that throne that occupied the holy of holies in the Jerusalem temple, which he knew about from his readings in the writings of Moses. True, Moses spoke of only two golden cherubim; Ezekiel saw four, but the boxlike configuration that he describes, and the overarching angelic wings touching each other, resemble the ark of the covenant. The fire and cloud that symbolize God's personal presence, as the apex of Ezekiel's vision, are strongly reminiscent of the Shekinah glory which appeared in the temple above the cherubim, whenever God wanted to indicate his special presence among his people.

It was a common belief among the Jews that the ark of the covenant was a copy, which Moses had made following precise divine instruction, of a real heavenly sanctuary. I believe that what Ezekiel saw, or thought he was seeing, at least, was a vision of that heavenly sanctuary. "The heavens were opened," he says (1:1). The veil of words and man-made depictions is for a moment lifted as Ezekiel is given a glimpse of the real thing, or at least as close to the real thing as any mortal eye can bear.

There is, however, one feature of this heavenly throne that Ezekiel is quite emphatic about but that finds no correlation either with the temple sanctuary or with previous visions of the divine glory such as Isaiah's. This throne, this ark, had castors.

As I looked at the living creatures, I saw a wheel on the ground beside each creature with its four faces. This was the appearance and structure of the wheels. They sparkled like chrysolite, and all four looked alike. Each appeared to be made like a wheel intersecting a wheel. As they moved, they would go in any one of the four directions the creatures faced; the wheels did not turn about as the creatures went. Their rims were high and awesome, and all four rims were full of eyes all around.

When the living creatures moved, the wheels beside them moved; and when the living creatures rose from the ground, the wheels also rose. Wherever the spirit would go, they would go, and the wheels would rise along with them, because the spirit of the living creatures was in the wheels. When the creatures moved, they also moved; when the creatures stood still, they also stood still; and when the creatures rose from the ground, the wheels rose along with them, because the spirit of the living creatures was in the wheels. (1:15-21)

The Jews' great spiritual danger at that time was that in losing contact with the temple they would feel deserted by God. They would feel that he who dwelt between the cherubim was remote from them. But now, in a single blast of prophetic illumination, Ezekiel sees that it is not so at all, for the ark in the temple was no more than a man-made replica. The real ark was infinitely more glorious. And it was mobile! God was not restricted to Jerusalem; he had moved to Babylonia, where his ailing people were.

This is the principal significance of this initial vision. Imagine the impact it must have made on Ezekiel. God was with the exiles wherever they were!

It seems to us self-evident that God is everywhere. But to the Jews at this stage of divine revelation, surrounded as they were by the notion that gods lived in shrines on mountaintops, it was a theological breakthrough of enormous importance. Without this knowledge, it would have been impossible for them to continue worshiping God in that foreign land. But with this new prophetic insight of Ezekiel's came the possibility of new expressions of Jewish piety that were not tied to a central system of worship. And so the synagogue was born. Such locally based worshiping communities would later be the model for the New Testament churches.

Without Ezekiel's insight the faith of Israel would always have been limited to Jewish culture and tradition. A God who is encountered only in Jerusalem can only be the God of the Jews. But Ezekiel's discovery that God was with the exiles constituted a huge step toward the universalizing of biblical religion.

Imagine too the personal spiritual encouragement that this revelation of God's presence must have brought to Ezekiel. His priestly vocation was not lost after all; God still had a vital job for him to do, even in the midst of a pagan society—a bigger job than he could have anticipated.

God's Servant Commissioned

I heard the voice of one speaking. He said to me, "Son of man, stand up on your feet and I will speak to you." As he spoke, the Spirit came into me and raised me to my feet, and I heard him speaking to me.

He said: "Son of man, I am sending you to the Israelites, to a rebellious nation that has rebelled against me; they and their ancestors have been in revolt against me to this very day. The people to whom I am sending you are obstinate and stubborn. Say to them, 'This is what the sovereign LORD says.' And whether they listen or fail to listen—for they are a rebellious house—they will know that a prophet has been among them." (1:28—2:5)

Some Christians entertain a romantic view of Christian ministry. How marvelous it must be, they say, to spend all your time praying and studying the Scriptures and helping people to know God! How incredibly fulfilling! There may be some truth in what they say, but it is a dangerous half-truth. It would be wise to weigh carefully and with sober realism the call that God communicates to those whom he appoints to prophetic office. Ezekiel is told here that his was an extremely difficult task. If he had been called to be a crosscultural missionary he would have had an easier job. We often have the idea the missionary who works overseas has a far more demanding role than the home-based pastor, and no doubt sometimes it is. But Ezekiel is told emphatically that it would not be so in his case:

You are not being sent to a people of obscure speech and difficult language, but to the house of Israel—not to many peoples of obscure speech and difficult language, whose words you cannot understand. Surely if I had sent you to them, they would have listened to you. But the house of Israel is not willing to listen to you because they are not willing to listen to me. (3:5-7)

In my own experience, the problems of trying to communicate God's word in a different language and culture are more than compensated for by the joy of working among spiritually responsive people who value one's ministry. But to have to preach to a spiritually hardened society, one's own flesh and blood, is almost unendurable. So while I pray for missionaries in Africa and in South America, I pray perhaps even more fervently for pastors who are working in the desolation of inner cities, or keeping a flickering light alive in an apathetic village, for they are the ones with the hardest task. Our neopagan, secular society is far harder ground to dig than the mission field in many parts of the world.

Ezekiel does of course experience certain compensations in this ministry. He finds satisfaction in being fed with God's word himself.

I looked, and I saw a hand stretched out to me. In it was a scroll, which he unrolled before me. On both sides of it were written words of lament and mourning and woe.

And he said to me, "Son of man, eat what is before you, eat this scroll; then go and speak to the house of Israel." So I opened my mouth, and he gave me the scroll to eat. (2:9—3:2)

This I take to be an eloquent picture of the nature of prophetic inspiration. Notice that the scroll is written on both sides, so there is no room for Ezekiel to add his own thoughts. This message is entirely the gift of God to him. It is one hundred percent divine in origin. Yet it must become subjectively his own before he can preach it to others. He must digest it, he must absorb it into the warmth and makeup of his own human personality. The word becomes one hundred percent human in that process of digestion.

Ezekiel tells us that the scroll was "as sweet as honey in my mouth" (3:3). In spite of the fact that its contents were lament and mourning and woe, the servant of God found a peculiar joy in preaching this divine word, a joy independent of the severity of the message, or even of the unresponsiveness of his audience. If his sermons blessed nobody else, Ezekiel's sermons at least seem to have blessed him.

The other compensation Ezekiel found in these early stages of his calling was the promise of protection, psychological and emotional.

> The house of Israel is not willing to listen to you because they are not willing to listen to me, for the whole house of Israel is hardened and obstinate. But I will make you as unyielding and hardened as they are. I will make your forehead like the hardest stone, harder than flint. Do not be afraid of them or terrified by them. (3:7-9)

Ezekiel would be strengthened to withstand the bullying he would have to endure in this situation. No doubt he felt weak and inadequate. But God would see to it that nothing could penetrate his spiritual armor. He would put steel into his spine. The prophets of the exile—Jeremiah, Ezekiel and Daniel—all had to be rugged individualists.

But neither the sweetness of the scroll nor the toughness of his forehead really disguises the unpalatable nature of the job he is being called to do. God is open with him: it is going to be lonely, uncomfortable and unsuccessful, he says. It will require physical courage because he will often feel intimidated. It will demand personal integrity because the temptation to be silenced by the spiritual resistance of the audience will be high: "You must speak my words to them, whether they listen or fail to listen" (2:7). It will require sustained commitment, because discouragement could easily breed surly resentment in the prophet himself: "But you, son of man, listen to what I say to you. Do not rebel like that rebellious house; open your mouth and eat what I give you" (2:8).

In these early experiences, Ezekiel is shown how emotionally draining his work is going to be.

> The Spirit lifted me up, and I heard behind me a loud rumbling sound—May the glory of the LORD be praised in his dwelling place!—the sound of the wings of the living creatures brushing against each other and the sound of the wheels beside them, a loud rumbling sound. The Spirit then lifted me up and took me away, and I went in bitterness and in the anger of my spirit, with the strong hand of the LORD upon me. (3:12-14)

Notice those words *bitterness* and *anger.* Some have interpreted this phrase to mean that Ezekiel was fed up with the job he had been given to do. But that is hardly the reason for the warning in 2:8 that he was to be a pliable and a willing servant in contrast with the rebelliousness of Israel. Nor does it accord with his sudden "Praise the Lord!" which precedes these words. It seems much more likely that this bitterness of spirit is an early example of something we find again and again in Ezekiel, and that is the way in which God's feelings about the situation are, so to speak, incarnated in the prophet's own emotional makeup. He was angry because the word he had received and absorbed into his heart was an angry word. The God before whose presence the angels bowed was a God whose heart was torn with disappointment and indignation, and Ezekiel identifies with God's heart.

So the word of God that is upon him inflames him. Indeed, he is rendered literally speechless by it for a while. "I came to the exiles who lived at Tel Abib. . . . I sat among them for seven days—overwhelmed" (3:15). Examples of this kind of emotional identification with the feelings of God in the situation are legion in the book of Ezekiel. It does not take much imagination to realize that such emotional engagement with the message would drain the man. All preachers experience this to some extent, but for a prophet it must have been greatly intensified.

God is also very frank about the formidable responsibility he was placing on this young man:

> Son of man, I have made you a watchman for the house of Israel; so hear the word I speak and give them warning from me. When I say to a wicked man, "You will surely die," and you do not warn him or speak out to dissuade him from his evil ways in order to save his life, that wicked man will die for his sin, and I will hold you accountable for his blood. (3:17-18)

A watchman is needed only in time of danger; he is the lookout who signals the approach of the invader so that the city is not taken by surprise. There is a profound irony about this particular watchman: he is being appointed by the enemy! It is God who is carrying out judgment against Israel. It is God who is Israel's foe at this time. That is the thrust of these early chapters. Yet it is God who puts the watchman in place and rings the alarm bell to warn of his hostile intent. What does this tell us about God? He is glorified in judgment, yet he never delights in the destruction of the wicked. His longing is always to exercise mercy. Luther said that wrath is God's strange work. It is alien to his nature, for wrath is not an eternal attribute of God in the way that love is. His wrath is called into existence by the phenomenon of sin, and it is quenched when sin is dealt with to his satisfaction. Love, on the other hand, is an innate divine energy that burns eternally among the persons of the Trinity. That is why the psalmist can say, "His anger lasts only a moment, but his favor lasts a lifetime" (Ps 30:5).

The fact that Ezekiel is hired by the very foe that he is supposed to be frustrating in no way mitigates the responsibility of the job. He is not just a token watchman. He has to fulfill his responsibility or pay for it: "I will hold you accountable for their blood." Watchmen are required to be alert to see the enemy, and faithful to blow the trumpet. The same two things are required of God's watchman. He must be alert to the divine word, rightly discerning what God is saying to his generation. He must not fill them with false hopes; he must not cry "Peace" when there is no peace; he must heed and understand the warning God is giving to an idolatrous people. Then he must be faithful in delivering it, in spite of unpopularity, in spite of the uncongenial nature of the message. He must diligently communicate that word, undistorted in its content and imperative in its tone. To fail to do so would implicate him in the fate of the wicked. To know that God's judgment must fall upon such a people, and to fail to do anything to avert it, is culpable negligence.

That surely represents the greatest challenge of these opening chapters to a faithful, believing people in a secular age. As we have seen, many in Ezekiel's day expected a speedy restoration of Israel to its former glories. But that was not the message God gave to Ezekiel, at least not in the short term. He did have something to say later about restoration, but Ezekiel's first word had to be a word of judgment, and that is significant. We must beware of ill-founded optimism. Premature talk of imminent revival may all too easily subvert the authentic word of God to an apostate church and to an idolatrous nation.

Our nation has rejected the faith of earlier generations in favor of the idols of modernity. The first word of a prophet to any such pagan world must be a word of judgment. The church, as salt of the earth and light of the world, has to be a watchman, rightly discerning what God's word against a sinful people is bound to be. The watchman issues a message of somber judgment upon the world and against the church, and it must be heard, not drowned out by our triumphalist choruses. The signs of that judgment are often to be seen in our daily newspapers and in our church periodicals. If the Christian community fails to perceive them, it will surely fail to be a watchman, and may even join the ranks of the false prophets who cried "Peace" when there was no peace. It may even turn out to be a watchman with blood on its hands.

Two

God's Glory with His People

EZEKIEL 8—11

*C*hurches die. Churches whose packed congregations once bustled with vitality, churches whose walls bear the names of godly pastors, churches that once saw remarkable revivals, today stand like empty barns. A few are kept open on Sundays by a handful of elderly people. Some have been turned into workshops or warehouses; others into temples or mosques. Some of these derelict sanctuaries bear names that testify to the optimism of earlier generations: Ebenezer (the stone of help), Bethesda (house of mercy), Rehoboth (broad places), Salem (peace), Bethel (house of God), Hope, Providence and, of course, Zion. But a more appropriate name for such churches would be that which the wife of Phineas gave to her son when she heard that the ark of the covenant had been captured by the Philistines. She named him Ichabod, because "the glory has departed" (1 Sam 4:21).

Why do churches die? Why does the glory sometimes depart from the people of God? In some parts of the world, such as in North Africa and some parts of Asia, entire Christian civilizations have been lost to rival ideologies and religions. Why?

Undoubtedly many factors are involved in the decline of churches, not the least of which is the inscrutable mystery of God's sovereign purpose. It would be grossly naive, if not a little arrogant, to attempt to analyze the highs and lows of church history in brief compass. But there can be no doubt that within the complex web of God's dealings with his people, one reason for the departure of God's blessing stands out. That reason is God's judgment.

Christ warned the church at Ephesus, "You have forsaken your first love. Remember the height from which you have fallen! Repent and do the things you did at first. If you do not repent, I will come to you and remove your lampstand from its place" (Rev 2:4-5). God is never irrevocably committed to any local shrine. As Ezekiel realized, he is not the God of places but the God of people. When those people persistently fail and do not repent, then no matter how ancient their traditions, no matter how sacred their church buildings, no matter how blessed their past history, Ichabod is their name. The glory will depart. That is the lesson of the chapters we shall look at now: Ezekiel 8—11. Here we see the glory of God departing and relocating elsewhere.

The Glory of God Offended

> In the sixth year, in the sixth month on the fifth day, while I was sitting in my house and the elders of Judah were sitting before me, the hand of the Sovereign LORD came upon me there. (8:1)

Remember the scene. Ezekiel is with the Jewish exiles in Babylonia. The year is now 591 B.C., and back in Jerusalem the situation is increasingly unstable. Zedekiah, the puppet king placed on the throne by the emperor Nebuchadnezzar, is under growing pressure from the populace to rebel against his imperial master and make a bid to restore Judah's national pride. Thus, they hope, he will fulfill all those prophecies of speedy restoration that are circulating. The exiles are concerned at disturbing reports of unsavory elements who are taking advantage of the lack of law and order in Jerusalem. What is going to happen? How will it affect them? News travels frustratingly slowly across those five hundred miles of desert. It is out-of-date before it arrives. *If only we could know what's going on now!* wish the exiles.

But maybe they can. *What about paying Ezekiel a call? He's a bit eccentric, but he does come from a good family, and people say he has an uncanny gift of telepathy. Maybe he can tune in to Jerusalem somehow and provide an up-to-date report of the current situation there.*

Such thinking seems to be the background to this delegation of senior men from the exilic community. They sat in front of the prophet wondering, with a mixture of foreboding and anticipation, whether he was going to have one of his odd turns. They were not left in doubt for very long.

The Idol That Provokes to Jealousy

I looked, and I saw a figure like that of a man. From what appeared to be his waist down he was like fire, and from there up his appearance was as bright as glowing metal. He stretched out what looked like a hand and took me by the hair of my head. The Spirit lifted me up between earth and heaven and in visions of God he took me to Jerusalem. (8:2-3)

Notice the phrase "in visions of God." This is not, as some have supposed, an example of psychic levitation, nor of conveyance by energy beam as in *Star Trek*. Ezekiel's body remained firmly exiled in Babylonia. It was only in visions, in his prophetic imagination, that he was transported. He did, however, seem to experience a rather uncomfortable physical sensation of high-speed travel, indicated by the expression "took me by the hair of my head." But what Ezekiel sees on arrival is far more hair-raising than the manner of his journey.

He took me . . . to the entrance to the north gate of the inner court, where the idol that provokes to jealousy stood. And

there before me was the glory of the God of Israel, as in the
vision I had seen in the plain.

   Then he said to me, "Son of man, look toward the north."
So I looked, and in the entrance north of the gate of the altar
I saw this idol of jealousy. (8:3-5)

Ezekiel already knew that it was the issue of idolatry that would
prove decisive in Judah's condemnation by God (see Ezekiel
4—7). The exile, he has heard, is a judgment from God, and the
judgment is not finished yet. Jerusalem is to suffer a permanent
and final fate. The terms "detestable idols" and "detestable
practices" had been burnt into his mind by repetition (5:9, 11;
6:9; 7:3-4, 8-9, 20). But perhaps even he had not realized to what
extent the idolatrous practices that God was condemning had
penetrated Jerusalem itself. As soon as he arrives in his vision he
is confronted by this ominous symbol, "the idol that provokes to
jealousy."

   Ezekiel uses a rather unusual word for *idol* here. It probably
denotes a replica of the carved wooden Asherah pole that King
Manasseh had erected some fifty years earlier (see 2 Kings 21).
It was a statue of a mother-goddess, a crude Canaanite fertility
symbol. Such images were not new in Israel, of course; the
prophets had been denouncing them for centuries. Indeed the
Asherahs are mentioned as early as the book of Judges (3:7). But
they were usually associated with rural peasantry. This obelisk of
obscenity, however, had been set up within the very temple
precincts, in full view of everyone who came to worship, including the king, who would regularly use the north gate to pass from
his royal palace into the temple area.

   Ezekiel's observation point is sited so as to convey the resulting
spiritual confrontation with maximum intensity. He stands inside the north gate. Looking north through the gate, he sees the
idol. Looking south from the gate, he sees hovering over the
inner sanctuary the Shekinah glory that symbolized God's presence. No wonder the Spirit calls it "the idol of jealousy." Yahweh,

the husband of Israel, joined to her by solemn covenant, had demanded her exclusive devotion. Yet, like a brazen hussy, she was openly making love to another in his own home, in his own direct line of vision, as it were. God could watch her infidelity through the gateway. The confrontation was as direct as that.

What does God see when he looks out through the doors of his churches today into our society? Perhaps the modern equivalent of an Asherah pole would be an adult bookstore, as they are euphemistically called. The mystery of sex, which Asherah personified and idolized, is still worshiped in such places. That worship is increasingly condoned publicly in our society, just as seems to have been the case in Jerusalem.

The Idolaters Among God's People

He said to me, "Son of man, do you see what they are doing— the utterly detestable things the house of Israel is doing here, things that will drive me far from my sanctuary? But you will see things that are even more detestable."

Then he brought me to the entrance to the court. I looked, and I saw a hole in the wall. He said to me, "Son of man, now dig into the wall." So I dug into the wall and saw a doorway there.

And he said to me, "Go in and see the wicked and detestable things they are doing here." (8:6-9)

Built into the temple walls were rooms generally occupied by important people in the national administration. Ezekiel is guided, it seems, through a hidden door into what might be termed an inner sanctum, had sanctity not been so conspicuously absent. For the walls of this secret chamber had been covered with frescoes depicting a veritable menagerie of pagan deities.

I went in and looked, and I saw portrayed all over the walls all kinds of crawling things and detestable animals and all the idols of the house of Israel. In front of them stood seventy elders of the house of Israel, and Jaazaniah son of Shaphan was standing among them. Each had a censer in his hand, and a fragrant cloud of incense was rising.

He said to me, "Son of man, have you seen what the elders of the house of Israel are doing in the darkness, each at the shrine of his own idol? They say, 'The LORD does not see us; the LORD has forsaken the land.' " (8:10-12)

The worship of animal deities in the ancient world was associated with Egypt. Could this clandestine gathering have had political overtones? Were the Jewish leaders plotting an alliance with Babylon's great imperial rival, Egypt? Had they given up on Yahweh and decided to court gods who might prove themselves more sympathetic to Judah's ambitions for a restored independence? This view is far from impossible. It would certainly explain the need for secrecy.

But I am tempted to think that this meeting was not quite as sinister as that. Notice the phrase "each at the shrine of his own idol." The emphasis is on the idiosyncratic nature of this idolatry. I do not believe this was a political conspiracy. It was much more like a private club where prominent men indulged their personal idolatrous inclinations without risking their public reputations.

The same goes on today: sophisticated, well-educated, well-dressed, respectable persons, obsessed like schoolchildren with secret societies, some in their Masonic lodges, some in their vice clubs, some in their black magic covens, and all enjoying the esoteric thrill of tasting forbidden fruit in their exclusive fraternities, and reassuring themselves that the Lord does not see them there.

Yet there is still more:

Again, he said, "You will see them doing things that are even more detestable."

Then he brought me to the entrance to the north gate of the house of the LORD, and I saw women sitting there, mourning for Tammuz. (8:13-14)

Usually it is the women who are the last to lose touch with real religion in a society. Perhaps they have a more intuitive feeling about spiritual things and are less reliant on the observable evidence of God's presence. Perhaps also motherhood makes them more sensitive to the moral welfare of their children than men sometimes are. When women stop praying, a society is really in trouble.

Tammuz was a Babylonian god, a handsome youth who, according to legend, died tragically. His story provided the focus for a cult of sentimentality that seems to have been particularly attractive to women at this time. Ezekiel sees tears that should have been shed for the sins of their husbands and children being squandered on this mythical Adonis.

Today those tears are more likely to be evoked by a romantic novel or a television soap opera, but I am not sure that there is any essential difference. Tammuz was a fantasy that provided these women with some emotional release from the tensions and realities of a rather austere life. In that respect it had much in common with the escapist entertainment that performs the same function in our society. Millions participate in the mythical world of *Melrose Place* or *ER* every week. Some years ago they were weeping for Bobby Ewing in *Dallas*. That may very well be a turn-of-the-century equivalent of weeping for Tammuz.

Ezekiel's vision is still not finished:

"Do you see this, son of man? You will see things that are even more detestable than this."

He then brought me into the inner court of the house of the LORD, and there at the entrance to the temple, between the portico and the altar, were about twenty-five men. With their backs toward the temple of the LORD and their faces toward the east, they were bowing down to the sun in the east. (8:15-16)

Step by step God has been bringing Ezekiel closer to the central sanctuary. First he saw the idol in the outer court, then the secret vault in the temple wall, then the women by the gate. Now his attention is drawn to a group of men who stand on the very threshold of the temple buildings. The implication seems to be that these were clergy. This area between the altar and the temple porch was the place where traditionally the priests stood to plead with God for the people's pardon. These men were standing there all right, but see which way they faced! Instead of facing the altar, they bowed toward the east. They worshiped the sun. They had literally turned their backs on God. So the clergy themselves were implicated in this horrendous slide toward national apostasy.

Cannot the same be said of many church leaders in our day? Have they not abandoned the exclusive claims of Christ for dialogue with other faiths and surrendered the authority of a trustworthy gospel in order to espouse the cause of rationalism and the so-called scientific study of the Bible? People who deny the deity of Christ or the authority of Scripture are ordained to the Christian ministry and even promoted to bishops' thrones or to chairs of theology. They have publicly turned their backs on the altar and yet retain office within the temple. God puts the same question to us as to Ezekiel:

> Have you seen this, son of man? Is it a trivial matter for the house of Judah to do the detestable things they are doing here? Must they also fill the land with violence and continually provoke me to anger? (8:17)

Is it trivial that sexual promiscuity is publicly condoned? Is it trivial that the nation's leadership indulges in occult vice? Is it trivial that the emotions of the populace are prostituted on escapist fantasies? Is it trivial that church leaders no longer believe the Apostles' Creed? Even if it seems trivial to us, it is not so to God. To him all these things are an unendurable provocation and the spiritual root from which stems the moral anarchy in our society. These detestable practices offend his glory.

That is probably the meaning of the rather difficult phrase at

the end of 8:17: "Look at them putting the branch to their nose!"
Some suggest that this refers to a mysterious pagan rite, but
perhaps those interpreters are nearer the mark who interpret
the Hebrew as meaning "They are a stench in my nose." The
glory of God dwells in the temple, or at least it should, yet all
around that temple and even within it lies the evidence of the
nation's unfaithfulness. Is it any wonder that God is repelled by
all this? Is it any wonder that the offended glory is on the point
of departure? "They are doing . . . things that will drive me far
from my sanctuary" (8:6).

Why are churches dying? Why has the spiritual health of our
land ebbed away? Why are the people of God in exile, feeling
marginalized? Here is one possible explanation: the glory of God
is a sensitive guest in any culture.

The Glory of God Avenged

Then I heard him call out in a loud voice, "Bring the guards
of the city here, each with a weapon in his hand." And I saw
six men coming from the direction of the upper gate, which
faces north, each with a deadly weapon in his hand. With them
was a man clothed in linen who had a writing kit at his side.
They came in and stood beside the bronze altar. (9:1-2)

These men are clearly not human soldiers. They are seven
archangels whose normal function is to defend God's people.
But they are taken from their normal duty on the city walls, and
given new orders. No longer are they commissioned to protect
Jerusalem. It is their duty now to execute judgment on it. Ezekiel
9 records the slaughter of the idolaters, and chapter 10 the
destruction of the city itself with holy fire.

We can note three points in chapter 9. First, the godly in the
city are afforded special protection.

Now the glory of the God of Israel went up from above the
cherubim, where it had been, and moved to the threshold of
the temple. Then the LORD called to the man clothed in linen

who had the writing kit at his side and said to him, "Go throughout the city of Jerusalem and put a mark on the foreheads of those who grieve and lament over all the detestable things that are done in it."

As I listened, he said to the others, "Follow him through the city and kill, without showing pity or compassion. Slaughter old men, young men and maidens, women and children, but do not touch anyone who has the mark." (9:3-6)

Ezekiel's imagery here has close links with that of the book of Revelation. In Revelation 7 the angels of wrath are not allowed to act until the servants of God have been sealed on their foreheads. Notice the criterion God instructs them to use in distinguishing those who may receive this mark of mercy. They "grieve and lament," he says, "over all the detestable things that are done in [Jerusalem]."

We cannot always prevent the slide toward apostasy in society or even in the visible church. God does not necessarily demand that we should. In totalitarian regimes, for instance, the power of government censorship and the use of police intimidation may silence all protest. Even in a democratic system, where freedom of speech may be guaranteed, there is no way that a few Christians can resist the paganizing majority indefinitely. But what God does expect of his faithful people in days of national, moral and spiritual degeneracy is dissent. He expects from us an emphatic mental repudiation of the values and practices of a paganizing world, a refusal to be conformed to it. More than dissent, he looks for a measure of disgust too: a deeply felt sense of horror and outrage at what is going on; a feeling of distress, grieving and lamenting. Remember Abraham's nephew, Lot? Though he lived in depraved Sodom, his spirit was vexed, his righteous soul was tormented, by the lawless deeds he saw and heard (2 Pet 2:7-8).

Here is an important truth. God is not impressed by Pharisees who think they can isolate themselves from judgment by living in the smug cocoon of their own self-righteousness, like prim virgins in a brothel. What God seeks are people who express their dissent and their moral outrage, not by sanctimonious prudery but by an agonizing sorrow of heart. Such people consciously recognize that there is a solidarity in sin, for human beings are social creatures and cannot sever themselves from the guilt of their neighbors. Rather, they feel ashamed and disgraced *with* their neighbors.

We shall not be judged solely on whether we have personally participated in sin but also on how we have responded to sin in our social environment. God's mark of redemption will be placed on those who grieve about it.

Second, notice the emotional burden that the premonition of judgment places on Ezekiel:

> Then he said to them, "Defile the temple and fill the courts with the slain. Go!" So they went out and began killing throughout the city. While they were killing and I was left alone, I fell facedown, crying out, "Ah, Sovereign LORD! Are you going to destroy the entire remnant of Israel in this outpouring of your wrath on Jerusalem?" (9:7-8)

The way Ezekiel dwells on the theme of judgment, describing it in such bloodcurdling terms, might lead us to think that he actually gained a sadistic pleasure from the subject. It is true that he is given such empathy with the mind of God that he shares a sense of holy satisfaction at the punishment of the wicked. But alongside that we have to set the witness of these verses where the prophet tells us he was appalled at the merciless slaughter he foresees. He expresses his sense of identification with the people under judgment. Everyone who ministers God's Word must suffer that tension as he or she stands between God and the people, hearing the Word of God from one side and the response of the people from the other. No one can preach judgment without praying for mercy. No one can speak to people about God without also speaking to God about people. If we do not feel that burden of intercession that moves us to cry, "Ah, Sovereign Lord!" it can only be because, unlike Ezekiel, we have not been left alone while the killing goes on in the streets outside.

Some commentators complain about Ezekiel's crude and bloody imagery of warrior angels with drawn swords. But it is only by painting such a barbaric and gory scene that the reality of judgment can be brought home to us with sufficient emotional force. This is another reason for those strange dramas that Ezekiel performs. He is concerned that we should not just think about his message but actually feel its reality.

Few of us have ever seen a massacre. Those who have served in the armed forces may know what a battlefield looks like. Most of us have seen grim reports of such scenes on the television news, or we have watched bloodthirsty films. Maybe the way to bring alive a passage like this for our generation is to take those images and multiply their intensity by a thousand. Then we may be close to feeling what we ought to feel about the nightmare of hell. It is not a matter for debate but a reality that must be felt. The plight of the lost should disturb us profoundly. It should drive us to our knees. If it does not, we have not yet seen what an awful thing it is to be lost.

The third point of chapter 3 is that when God judges the world he does not begin with the Muslims or the Buddhists or the Hindus. Judgment starts with the visible churches: " 'Begin at my sanctuary.' So they began with the elders who were in front of the temple" (9:6). "Who can endure the day of his coming?" says Malachi (3:2). For it is to the people of God that he will come first. That brings us back to our initial question: Why do churches die? The death of churches is the first sign of a society under judgment, the first indication that the glory is departing.

The Glory Relocated

Then the Spirit lifted me up and brought me to the gate of the house of the LORD that faces east. There at the entrance to the gate were twenty-five men, and I saw among them Jaazaniah son of Azzur and Pelatiah son of Benaiah, leaders of the people. The LORD said to me, "Son of man, these are the men who are plotting evil and giving wicked advice in this city. They say, 'Will it not soon be time to build houses? This city is a cooking pot, and we are the meat.' Therefore prophesy against them; prophesy, son of man." (11:1-4)

What evil were these men plotting? Their cryptic words do not tell us very clearly. Perhaps they were a political pressure group, advocating rebellion against Babylonia—members of that secret seventy who conspired in the temple wall. If that is the case, they are saying something like "Jerusalem is a secure city. It's never going to be conquered. Like meat in the caldron, we're safe from the flames of Babylonian aggression because we're on the inside of this sacred city. There's a cast-iron barrier around us. So now is the time to make a bid for the restoration of our national prosperity and independence."

Another ingenious suggestion links this crowd with the prophecy of Jeremiah. Though he is never mentioned in Ezekiel, Jeremiah was a senior contemporary of Ezekiel and was ministering in the city of Jerusalem at this time. At some point during the period between the first and second deportations, Jeremiah wrote an open letter to the exiles, among whom was Ezekiel. One of Jeremiah's instructions to them from the Lord was "Build houses and settle down" in Babylonia (Jer 29:5). Some commentators think that this group of leaders in Jerusalem is directly contradicting the advice of Jeremiah. "This is not a time to build houses in Babylon," they are saying. "We're not going to go into exile; we're going to overthrow Babylonia!"

There may be truth in both those interpretations, but the evidence suggests a third. Verse 6 says, "You have killed many people in this city and filled its streets with the dead." This does not sound like political activists plotting revolution. I suspect they were just a gang of opportunist criminals, taking advantage

of the lawless state into which Jerusalem had fallen since Babylonia deported the cream of its national leadership. On that
reading, the twenty-five men are saying that the exiles are just
the bones and the giblets which fate has thrown on the scrap-
heap. They, on the other hand, are the juicy meat, about to grow
fat through building houses out of the wealth the exiles had left
behind. Either way, the question at issue is not so much the
advisability of rebellion against Babylon as which group of Jews
God was going to bless during this period. Would it be those who
had gone into exile, or the residual population in Jerusalem?
This group of men clearly represented those who felt that God
was still on the side of the Jews who remained in Jerusalem. These
twenty-five tough guys believed that the future lay with them.

Ezekiel's message is the exact opposite: "This city will not be
a pot for you," says God, "nor will you be the meat in it; I will
execute judgment on you at the borders of Israel" (11:11). This
verdict is immediately confirmed and emphasized when one of
these brigands is struck dead on the spot (11:13). This interpretation also makes sense of verses 14-16:

> The word of the LORD came to me: "Son of man, your broth-
> ers—your brothers who are your blood relatives and the whole
> house of Israel—are those of whom the people of Jerusalem
> have said, 'They are far away from the LORD; this land was
> given to us as our possession.'
>
> "Therefore say: 'This is what the Sovereign LORD says:
> Although I sent them far away among the nations and scat-
> tered them among the countries, yet for a little while I have
> been a sanctuary for them in the countries where they have
> gone.' "

This gang that was trying to seize power in Jerusalem took the
line that God had deserted the exiles and that Jerusalem was the
place where the blessings belonged. But God says that it is to the
exiles that Israel must look for its future. No one in Jerusalem
can help the nation now. The exiles are the ones God is deter-

mined to bless, not that lawless and corrupt gang of idolaters who hope to line their pockets out of the misfortune of their exiled compatriots. God is here, in Babylonia, in this new, uncongenial, pagan society into which the exiles have been thrown. Believe it or not, that is where God's purposes for the future lie.

Babylon: Focus of Hope

This theme of Babylon, rather than Jerusalem, as the focus of hope underlies the strange movements of the Shekinah glory which Ezekiel reports throughout chapters 9—11. At the commencement of the judgment by slaughter, "the glory of the God of Israel went up from above the cherubim, where it had been, and moved to the threshold of the temple" (9:3). It leaves the carved cherubim on the ark and moves to the edge of the temple building, the threshold. Then at the end of the judgment by slaughter, Ezekiel "saw the likeness of a throne of sapphire above the expanse that was over the heads of the cherubim. The LORD said to the man clothed in linen, 'Go in among the wheels beneath the cherubim'" (10:1-2).

In other words, this strange wheeled platform, which Ezekiel saw in his initial vision, has reappeared. The mobile throne has come onto the scene again. After the judgment by fire, "the glory of the LORD departed from over the threshold of the temple and stopped above the cherubim" (10:18). So the glory leaves the temple threshold and hovers over its heavenly chariot. "While I watched, the cherubim spread their wings and rose from the ground, and as they went, the wheels went with them. They stopped at the entrance to the east gate of the LORD's house, and the glory of the God of Israel was above them" (10:19). So the glory now moves to the door of the sanctuary area, to the east gate of the outer court.

The meaning of all these movements is quite clear. God is leaving the sanctuary. He has seen what is going on in the temple area; he goes to the door of the sanctuary, summons his wheeled vehicle, mounts it and departs.

Where is the glory of the Lord going? Notice by which gate he leaves—the east gate. What lay to the east? Babylon! God was going to join the exiles, as indeed Ezekiel already knew. The prophet had already encountered this heavenly juggernaut, not in Jerusalem but by the River Kebar, where the exiles were encamped. And if we are in any doubt about the matter, 11:22-24 seals the issue:

> Then the cherubim, with the wheels beside them, spread their wings, and the glory of the God of Israel was above them. The glory of the LORD went up from within the city and stopped above the mountain east of it. The Spirit lifted me up and brought me to the exiles in Babylonia in the vision given by the Spirit of God.

Jerusalem, then, was no longer the spiritual center of the people of God. The glory of God had been temporarily relocated in a foreign land, and Jerusalem had been abandoned.

God on the Move Today

What are the implications of this for us as we live in a pagan land ourselves, where church membership has been falling, and where the public influence of Christianity has been declining for many years and continues to do so in spite of talk of imminent revival?

When churches die as a result of God's judgment on their spiritual decline, it may be wise to look around to see what new thing is happening outside the old structures of the visible church. Whatever reservations we may have about some of the newer groups that have arisen in the restorationist movement and the charismatic movement generally, they highlight one fact that we cannot afford to neglect: God is never tied to established structures. Sometimes when the church abandons its spiritual heritage, repudiates the truth of the gospel, fails to evangelize the nation as it should and rejects the role God has given it, it may well be that God deserts the institutions of the past. It is certainly true that revivals in the past often required new structures. Many revivals were not church-based but happened despite the reluctance of the traditional churches.

God is mobile. He is not the God of places but the God of people. That is the message of the exile. The fact that a church is long established does not guarantee it a permanent title to the glory of God. He is always our living contemporary. Our problem is to keep up with what he is doing. He is always one step ahead of his church.

We live in a secularized society like those exiles. Perhaps we should learn to accept that fact and adapt ourselves to the new social realities, rather than waste time romanticizing the good old days.

It may be that God is more concerned about the spiritual caliber of his people than the visible evidence of their prosperity in the eyes of the world. And he is prepared to sacrifice the latter for the sake of the former.

This is what the Sovereign LORD says: "I will gather you from the nations and bring you back from the countries where you have been scattered, and I will give you back the land of Israel again.

"They will return to it and remove all its vile images and detestable idols. I will give them an undivided heart and put a new spirit in them; I will remove from them their heart of stone and give them a heart of flesh." (11:17-19)

If churches die, then, it may sometimes be for the long-term good of the whole church. We ought not to be sentimental about the closure of churches. The day may come when new fellowships will be built by a people more spiritually motivated than those who presided over their decline.

The greatest need of the people of God is not church buildings, or even the visible means of grace, but spiritual vitality: "I will . . . put a new spirit in them. . . . Then they will follow my decrees and be careful to keep my laws. They will be my people, and I will be their God" (11:19-20). Here is a prophecy of a chastened and purified people. It points forward to One who would baptize not with water but with the Holy Spirit and with fire, bringing forth a spiritual regeneration.

Two further observations on these chapters are rather provocative. What was the mark that was to be put on the foreheads of those who grieved for the sins of Jerusalem (9:4)? Some of the older commentators point out that the letter denoting the mark in the ancient Hebrew script was actually in the shape of a cross. One hesitates to read too much into that, but it is a little tantalizing. The other observation concerns the mountain to the east of Jerusalem, where the glory of the Lord hovered as it departed (11:23). There is another name for that hill—the Mount of Olives. There seems to be a certain wistfulness as the glory of God looks back from that mountain. Five centuries later, of course, the glory would leave Jerusalem from that same point once again, this time not on a throne but tabernacled in a body of glorified humanity, and this time not in judgment but in blessing. "Surely I am with you always, to the very end of the age," he would say (Mt 28:20).

Yes, churches may die, but the redeemed of the Lord need not despair. God still has his purposes for his people. That is what Ezekiel had to learn. We must beware of short-term optimism that short-circuits the judgment of God that will fall on an apostate society and on an apostate church. But we must not underestimate the fact that God may already be sowing the seeds of something new to restore his people, constructing perhaps a new way of being the people of God, even in an exilic situation.

One of the things we shall learn later from Daniel is how the people of God were to cope practically during that exilic period. Daniel holds before us the long-term hope that whether revival comes or not, the kingdom of God will not be defeated. God's purposes for his people are secure.

Some of us may belong to churches that are doing well. We feel encouraged. But more of us, I suspect, are in churches where there is more than a little discouragement, more than a little sense of struggling in a society that seems reluctant to respond to the message of the gospel. In spite of talk of imminent revival, we do not see a great deal of it in our communities. The signs of hope are there, perhaps more now than ten years ago. But it is nothing like the revival that took place in the eighteenth century, or at the beginning of the twentieth in some parts of the United States and British Isles. For those of us who must wrestle with the reality of the church in exile, perhaps Ezekiel's vision of the departing glory, for all its pessimism and sadness, is a vision we need to take on board. For when "Ichabod" is written over the structures of the past, it may very well be that God is planning something new for the future.

Three

A Challenge to Comfortable Christians

EZEKIEL 12—14

*H*ave you ever seen a pet rock? I met one some years ago. An American student in Cambridge was not allowed to keep a dog or cat in college, so he kept a smoothly polished rock instead. It sat on his bedside table where he could stroke it, especially when he felt lonely and far from home. He said it gave him a secure feeling.

Have you ever seen a pet Bible? People do keep Bibles as pets, and they usually sit on their bedside tables too. Every night they fondle its pages, reading a favorite verse or two to comfort and relax them before they go to sleep. By this means they think they are maintaining a relationship with God. Unfortunately, for all the practical difference it makes to their lives, they might just as well stroke a rock as the leather of their Bible. For their Bible never roars or snarls at them. It purrs soothingly in their hands and makes them feel safe and happy. It is domesticated and tame.

The Jews, at the time of the exile, tended to treat their Bible in that way. That was one of the reasons the judgment of God was coming upon them so inexorably. Yet they were unaware of it. They wanted the comfort and security of the prophetic word without having to face up to its disquieting challenge to their lifestyle. So they found ways of controlling that word, muzzling its bark, domesticating it.

That Doesn't Apply to Us!

Those who have reservations about using drama as an ally to preaching may well find themselves challenged by the way Ezekiel acts out his message. Back in chapters 4 and 5 there are a number of examples of this. He draws a visual aid to serve as a backdrop to his stage production and erects miniaturized items of battle in a way that comes close to puppetry. Then he engages in a kind of mime tableau, first playing the role of God by attacking the city, and then portraying the sufferings of the people under siege within it. After that comes that piece of slapstick to which I referred in chapter one, in which he waves a sword around and cuts off his beard.

He uses such techniques in order to overcome the complacency of his congregation. In their remote situation the exiles found it hard to believe that Jerusalem was in grave danger. They were comfortable. So he acts out the imminent judgment on Jerusalem in order to bring its reality home to them. The visual is often much more emotionally powerful than the oral. We can cope with news of famine when we hear it on the radio, but when we see images of starving children on television we reach for our checkbooks. Ezekiel gives his audience the maximum opportunity to engage with the terror of the events that were to take place.

In the opening verses of chapter 12, we find him engaged in another visual drama. This time he makes a big show of packing his bags and burrowing out through the wall of his house, rather than using the front door. Then he staggers off blindfolded through the street.

It is not hard to imagine the amused chuckles of his mystified audience. What on earth is the madman up to this time? Drama often provokes a laugh—at first. The next morning he wipes the smile off their faces by telling them what it all meant.

In the morning the word of the LORD came to me: "Son of man, did not that rebellious house of Israel ask you, 'What are you doing?'

"Say to them, 'This is what the Sovereign LORD says: This oracle concerns the prince in Jerusalem and the whole house of Israel who are there.' Say to them, 'I am a sign to you.'

"As I have done, so it will be done to them. They will go into exile as captives.

"The prince among them will put his things on his shoulder at dusk and leave, and a hole will be dug in the wall for him to go through. He will cover his face so that he cannot see the land. I will spread my net for him, and he will be caught in my snare; I will bring him to Babylonia, the land of the Chaldeans, but he will not see it, and there he will die. I will scatter to the winds all those around him—his staff and all his troops—and I will pursue them with drawn sword." (12:8-14)

The prince in question is Zedekiah, the puppet king whom Nebuchadnezzar had left on the throne of Jerusalem when he took Jehoiachin and the rest of the Jewish aristocracy into exile in the first deportation. Having previously acted out the horrors of the coming siege of Jerusalem, Ezekiel now portrays the way Zedekiah would try to escape from that beleaguered city. This actually happened some three years later. There is a remarkable degree of correspondence between the historical accounts of the failed escape and this dramatic representation of it by the prophet (compare this passage with 2 Kings 25:1-7 and Jeremiah 39:1-7). Zedekiah did indeed break through the city wall under cover of night in his endeavor to escape. He was indeed spotted and overwhelmed by the Babylonian troops surrounding the city. The troops he had taken with him did desert. The cryptic comment about his coming to Babylonia and dying there, and yet not seeing it, is clarified by what subsequently happened: the Babylonians, as a punishment for his rebellion, blinded him (having first executed his sons in front of him) and then brought him to Babylon.

This was not at all the sort of message that the Jews in exile wanted to hear, nor did Ezekiel do anything to reassure their disturbed minds. He followed up this carefully dramatized prison breakout with a graphic demonstration of theatrical emotion.

> Son of man, tremble as you eat your food, and shudder in fear as you drink your water. Say to the people of the land: "This is what the Sovereign LORD says about those living in Jerusalem and in the land of Israel: They will eat their food in anxiety and drink their water in despair, for their land will be stripped of everything in it because of the violence of all who live there." (12:18-19)

How would his audience react to all this? Even before the curtain went up, so to speak, God had warned Ezekiel not to be disappointed if their response was negative. "Son of man, you are living among a rebellious people. They have eyes to see but do not see and ears to hear but do not hear, for they are a rebellious people" (12:2). So there never was much hope that Ezekiel's enactments would change them. That is why God continues: "Therefore, son of man, pack your belongings for exile. . . . Perhaps they will understand, though they are a rebellious house" (12:3).

That word *perhaps* contains an important lesson for us. We may often be deterred in evangelism by lack of results. What's the point of talking to this person about Christ? She always shrugs it off. What's the point of sending missionaries back there? Nobody's ever been converted. It's a waste of time and effort. Perhaps it is. But the Word must still be preached as long as that "perhaps" remains. For God's Word is never wasted. It accomplishes its purpose—if not in salvation, then in judgment. Ezekiel says many, many times in this prophecy, "Then they will know that I am the LORD" (e.g., 12:16). If they will not know him through experiencing his mercy, they will know him through experiencing his judgment. The Word must still be preached, then, even in difficult and unresponsive places. We must not allow personal discouragement or pessimistic fatalism to extinguish that "perhaps."

In Ezekiel's case the "perhaps" did not materialize, for all his visual and verbal efforts. The people wanted a pet Bible, a Bible that ignored their failures and confirmed them in their false hopes. Notice the way they handled Ezekiel's prophecy in order to domesticate it. Some of them responded with rank skepticism. As they listened to Ezekiel's grim message, they bandied about a saying: "The days go by and every vision comes to nothing" (12:22). In Hebrew it is just four words, cleverly put together like an advertising slogan, so that it sticks in the mind. Perhaps the nearest equivalent in English is "Tomorrow never comes." Doomsayers, they said, have been proclaiming that the end of the world is nigh for years. But it hasn't happened yet. Ezekiel is just another crank; it is not worth taking him seriously.

Others, however, seem to have felt it was far too risky to reject a prophecy out of hand in that contemptuous way, so instead they resorted to evasive interpretation: "The vision he sees is for many years from now, and he prophesies about the distant future" (12:27). They did not question Ezekiel's prophetic inspiration, but they did not see it as relevant to them. It was a prophecy for the very long-term future.

In both these ways, skepticism and false interpretation, Ezekiel's audience took the line that "this doesn't apply to us." They heard the word of God without practically responding to it.

In the same way, people today bring their pet Bible to heel when it threatens to pull on the leash. When they read a passage they do not like, what do they do?

Some simply deny its inspiration. "This is a copyist's error," they say, "or an editorial gloss; or the author made a mistake." Others, not quite so bold, interpret the passage in such a way as to remove its disturbing implications: "You can't take that literally," they will say, or "It was relevant to their culture but not to ours." Thus they refuse to apply the text to themselves, preferring to hold on to their preconceived ideas rather than have them challenged by the Word of God.

Perhaps no area of truth suffers more from that kind of Bible study than the doctrine of the last things. As the apostle Peter would later write, people do not relish talk of the imminent return of Christ to judge the world. They scoff at it: "Where is this 'coming' he promised? Ever since our fathers died, everything goes on as it has since the beginning of creation" (2 Pet 3:4). It is exactly the same excuse.

God's answer to such avoidance tactics is the one he gave the Jews through Ezekiel: "Therefore say to them, 'This is what the Sovereign LORD says: None of my words will be delayed any longer; whatever I say will be fulfilled, declares the Sovereign LORD'" (12:28). If we do not apply God's Word to our lives, the day will come when it will be applied to us, whether we like it or not.

"Let's Go and Hear the Reverend Whitewash Instead"

The word of the LORD came to me: "Son of man, prophesy against the prophets of Israel who are now prophesying. Say to those who prophesy out of their own imagination: 'Hear the word of the LORD! This is what the Sovereign LORD says: Woe to the foolish prophets who follow their own spirit and have seen nothing!' " (13:1-3)

Ezekiel belonged to a prophetic tradition in Israel that went back for centuries. Ever since the days of the judges, training colleges, or schools for "the sons of the prophets," had prepared young men for the prophetic office. Samuel sent the newly anointed King Saul on a crash course at one (1 Sam 10:1-13). Unfortunately, with the passage of the years, a spiritual deterioration had blighted these academies. Their graduates still called themselves "sons of the prophets," but the message they brought was a fake.

As Ezekiel is told here quite candidly, they prophesy out of their own imagination; they follow their own spirit; they have seen nothing. As a result, their visions are false.

The seriousness of this fraud cannot be overstated. The Bible is God's revelation. The whole structure of its message stands on the conviction that God has spoken through the prophets. Therefore we are not at liberty to choose what we believe. The word *heresy* is derived from the Greek word that means "to choose." A heretic is someone who chooses what to believe.

"What's wrong with that?" many would say. "We've all got a right to our own religious opinions." That of course, is nonsense. We have no right whatsoever to any religious opinions. That is precisely the sin forbidden in the second commandment, "You shall not make for yourself an idol" (Ex 20:4). It is the hallmark of idolaters that they choose what sort of God to believe in. "I think God is like . . ." Such a god originates in human imagination. But we may not invent God; we must submit to God as he reveals himself to be. Christianity is a religion not of human speculation but of divine disclosure. All our choices in matters of faith are therefore constrained by revelation.

Christian teachers may be original in their presentation of the truth. They may be imaginative in their application of the truth. But when it comes to the fundamental *content* of the truth, they must be plagiarists. Heresy is simply theological originality. Christian theology is a science based on data, not a creative exercise in free composition. It is a science, not an art. Those who fail to understand this fact sin with their intellects as seriously as adulterers sin with their bodies. We may not choose to do with our bodies what God says to be wrong, and we may not believe with our minds what God states to be false. We can no more choose our own religious opinions than we can choose our own moral code. In both, our conscience is bound to the Word of God. This fundamental humility is required of anybody who wants to be a Christian, and certainly of anybody who wants to be a Christian communicator. But these so-called prophets did not see it that way.

True prophets knew that it was not by their own theological genius that they helped people to know more of God. Rather, they were channels of divine revelation, which they received consciously through a unique prophetic experience. We do not share that experience, and consequently it is hard for us to understand. Sometimes the prophets compare it to hearing (they receive a word from God) and sometimes to seeing (they are granted a vision of God). However this revelation was communicated to them, they were never in any doubt about its divine origin. They had not dreamed it up. It did not derive from their own mind. It had come to them, and with an objectivity that excluded all self-doubt and enabled them to say, "This is what the Lord says." That was their chief credential in presenting their message as authoritative: a distinctive, supernatural, prophetic consciousness.

Since the experience was a private one, however, it was possible to lay fraudulent claim to it, and by the period of the exile that was indeed happening. People such as Jeremiah and Ezekiel, who had been burdened with an authentic word from God, found themselves contradicted by false prophets. Not that these impostors deliberately tricked their hearers; there is a frightening hint that these people were self-deceived. "They say, 'The LORD declares,' when the LORD has not sent them; yet they expect their words to be fulfilled" (13:6). It was not, then, that they were insincere in what they said. They really expected their words to be fulfilled. But there is such a thing as wishful thinking. If the true prophet saw visions, these false prophets saw visions, or at least they said they did. If the true prophets said, "This is what the Lord says," so did the false prophets. It seems they really believed that this *was* what the Lord was saying; this *was* what was going to happen. In every respect their outward appearance was indistinguishable from the genuine article. There was no simple external test, then, by which to unmask these people. They made exactly the same claims as the true prophets did.

How to Spot False Prophets

Ezekiel gives us a few clues that will enable us to identify these false prophets.

Character. "Foolish prophets," he calls them. *Foolish* is a strong word in Hebrew. It is a comment not so much on their intellectual ability as on their moral caliber. Fools did not fear God. Boorish and arrogant, they opened their mouths too wide too often. There was no grace, no humility in the fool. These prophets were like that.

Motivation. They were "like jackals among ruins" (13:4). Far from offering Israel any constructive help, they were further undermining it, like vermin burrowing in the debris. They were exploiting the situation for their own gain: "You have profaned me among my people for a few handfuls of barley and scraps of bread" (13:19). In other words, they were professionals. They were in it for the money.

Religious quacks always multiply in days of national crisis. Like spiritual parasites, they make a living off people's spiritual hunger. "In their greed," says Peter, "these teachers will exploit you with stories they have made up" (2 Pet 2:3). These false prophets similarly made a commercial enterprise of God's people. Indeed, one way of identifying false prophecy and heresy is to look at the financial interests involved. This may seem rather cynical, but many of the questionable cults and sects that have arisen in recent decades would have been exposed much earlier if their accounts had been examined. Where is the money coming from? More important, where is it going? Religion is big business. When Peter speaks of the "experts in greed" who "have left the straight way and wandered off," his Old Testament example is the false prophet Balaam, who "loved the wages of wickedness" (2 Pet 2:14-15).

Methodology. The word *divinations* (13:6) is a technical word meaning the obtaining of an oracle by reading omens, and in the Old Testament it is often associated with witchcraft. It seems likely that these false prophets have strayed into the arena of occultism and have embraced essentially pagan methods of foreseeing the future. This seems to be borne out by Ezekiel's prophecy against "the daughters of your people who prophesy out of their own imagination . . . the women who sew magic charms on all their wrists and make veils of various lengths for their heads in order to ensnare people" (13:17-18). As in the spiritualist church of today, these prophets were blending biblical religion with occult practice. In particular, they seem to have been running a kind of protection racket, trading on people's fear. They sold them talismans and good-luck charms to ward off ill fortune. "You want to be prosperous? You want things to go well? We'll give you a favorable prediction if you pay us enough."

Content of their preaching. "They lead my people astray, saying, 'Peace,' when there is no peace, and . . . when a flimsy wall is built, they cover it with whitewash" (13:10). The authentic prophetic word is always first a word of warning, a word of judgment. This is invariably so in the Bible. Only secondarily, when people have taken that warning on board, is it a word of hope. The great prophets of the Old Testament do not issue words of hope until the people have been reduced to hopelessness by the word of judgment. The trumpet blast of the watchman, warning the city of imminent disaster, is the hallmark of the true prophet, says Ezekiel. By contrast, the message of the false prophets is invariably one of complacency and optimism. Good times are coming, they say. Instead of exposing the cracks in the wall, they disguise them with whitewash. Instead of denouncing the false hopes of God's people as they trust luck and refuse to face up to the coming judgment, they sanctify them with the whitewash of religious language. Instead of calling people to repent, they confirm them in the lie.

> Because you disheartened the righteous with your lies, when I had brought them no grief, and because you encouraged the wicked not to turn from their evil ways and so save their lives, therefore you will no longer see false visions or practice divination. (13:22-23)

Francis Schaeffer called the false prophet an "echo of the world." That is a good description, for false prophets are always endorsing the current trend. Their goal is popularity, not integrity. They want to know how many are going to come and listen. The easiest way to be popular is to baptize the current trend, to jump on the bandwagon, to say what people want you to say. In a permissive age, therefore, the false prophets preach situation ethics: "Do whatever seems most loving." In an authoritarian age they are Pharisees: "Follow the rules, down to the last detail." In a conservative age they support the status quo; in a revolutionary age they want to overthrow it. In a rationalist age they are intellectuals; in a mystical age they are gurus. The one thing false prophets never ask anybody to do is to change. They have words of comfort, never of challenge; of endorsement, never of contradiction; of compromise, never of principle; and always of hope, never of judgment. "Peace," they say, even though there is no peace.

These false prophets, then, could be distinguished by their character, motivation, methods and teaching. Ultimately, too, says Ezekiel, they are distinguishable by the verdict of history upon them.

> My hand will be against the prophets who see false visions and utter lying divinations. They will not belong to the council of my people or be listed in the records of the house of Israel, nor will they enter the land of Israel. Then you will know that I am the Sovereign LORD. (13:9)

In the long run it will be the Jeremiahs and the Ezekiels that God will vindicate, for all their unpopularity among their contemporaries. It is their writings that have come down to us today in the canon of Scripture, not those of the false prophets. Usually we do not even know their names.

All these characteristics, then, mark out false prophets for what they are. But sadly, the people were not interested in their exposure. They wanted a pet Bible, a Bible that said only what they wanted to hear. False prophets gave them exactly such a Bible. The sermons of the Reverend Whitewash and his colleagues were so much easier to listen to than Ezekiel's.

It is through listening to the ministry of our contemporary false prophets, of course, that countless men and women today succeed in domesticating the Bible. Instead of being confronted from the pulpit by the roar of a lion, they meet only the purr of a kitten. In some churches they hear comfortable little homilies that disturb nobody, offend nobody and, of course, convert nobody. In others, they are entertained by multimedia spectacles that thrill and excite as much as a visit to the movie theater. They enjoy it. It is what they want to hear.

The greatest threat to the kingdom of God is always internal, not external. It was not really Babylon that defeated Judah. It was the flimsiness of its own defenses, whitewashed over by the false prophets. "They lead my people astray, saying, 'Peace,' when there is no peace. . . . When the wall collapses, will people not ask you, 'Where is the whitewash you covered it with?'" (13:10-12). This is so often what happens. Eventually disillusionment comes, but it is too late for a remedy. If we encourage false hope in a world in which there is no true hope, then we simply invite disenchantment in the long term. Faith built on a false hope is bound to collapse. Milton pictures it graphically in *Lycidas:*

The hungry sheep look up, and are not fed,
But swoln with wind and the rank mist they draw,
Rot inwardly and foul contagion spread;
Besides what the grim wolf with privy paw
Daily devours apace, and nothing said.

The flock is thus decimated by such false shepherds. We do people no favors by giving them false hopes. As Milton comments in the lines that are perhaps the best-known of the same passage,

That two-handed engine at the door
Stands ready to smite once, and smite no more.

The reference is, of course, to the sword of judgment, the

awesome, two-handed weapon of God's destruction.

True and False Prophets Today

What does all this mean for us? First, we must overcome our natural gullibility. The trouble with us Christians is that we are too easygoing. We find it hard to believe that that nice man with the clergy collar and the letters after his name could be a false prophet. We are so easily duped by the sheep's clothing. We need to be critical of the sermons we hear and the books we read. The false prophets may well be clever and effective in their publicity; they may well have qualifications and dress up in ecclesiastical vestments; they may well exhibit prophetic ecstasy, as Ezekiel's false prophets seem to have done. We must weigh what they say.

Second, we must be prepared to separate from false teachers when occasion demands it. Like Ezekiel, we must publicly dissociate ourselves from error, even when it is taught by ministers in our own churches. In Ezekiel's day the situation was so grave that he had to preach against the preachers, to prophesy against the prophets. It was a terrible thing for God to have to say. But Christianity is bound to be a controversial religion. We must not draw back from polemical debate when necessary; we must not be afraid to contradict wrong doctrine. For all the pain this may cause, and for all our desire for unity, the lie has to be exposed as a lie.

Third, we must support those who teach God's truth, regardless of denomination or emphasis. If Ezekiel were to visit our church today, many of us would probably regard him as an extreme charismatic. He had bizarre visions and used drama a lot. He was far from what a good conservative evangelical ought to look like and sound like! But he was on the side of the truth. Where were the people of goodwill who should have aligned themselves with him? Why did he have to be such a lonely voice? He was a bit odd, cranky even, and those who associated with him would probably have been regarded with the same suspicion. But did he not deserve support from those who were for the God of Israel?

Finally, those of us who have any teaching responsibility in the church must examine our own ministry. It is easy for an evangelical Christian, reading Ezekiel 13, to feel complacent. The false prophets of today are often easy to spot. We might think of the cults, such as the Moonies and the Jehovah's Witnesses, and then the liberal theologians who deny the authority of Scripture. We might add anybody else we dislike or disagree with! These obvious examples, however, might blind us to the more subtle forms of false prophecy within our own camp. What characterized Ezekiel's false prophets was not just that they preached lies but that they preached what people wanted to hear. They were not necessarily deliberate deceivers. They thought they were doing a good job. But they were comfortable preachers who confirmed their hearers in their preconceived ideas. They were conventional preachers who never risked their public acceptability by saying anything unpopular.

If anything deserves the title *conservative*, isn't it this? Were not the false prophets decidedly conservative? It worries me when people nod too vigorously in agreement with my sermons. That is exactly the reaction the false prophets got to their sermons. It worries me that too much evangelical preaching is boringly predictable, for the false prophets were boringly predictable too. Trite formulas and glib clichés come to our lips far too easily. Evangelical preaching can be very smug and self-assured. Surely a prophetic word ought to disturb us, surprise us, shock us and send us away feeling decidedly uncomfortable, maybe even angry or upset. If our teaching lacks that cutting edge, then no matter how apparently orthodox or sound it may be, it is certainly not prophecy.

Let us sit under the ministry of the Reverend Whitewash, then, if we prefer our Bible tame and comforting.

What Do You Mean? We're Evangelicals!

> Some of the elders of Israel came to me and sat down in front
> of me. Then the word of the LORD came to me: "Son of man,
> these men have set up idols in their hearts and put wicked
> stumbling blocks before their faces. Should I let them inquire
> of me at all?" (14:1-3)

Here is a group of important people who clearly want to be
known as spiritual and who seek to obtain such a reputation for
themselves by patronizing Ezekiel's pulpit. They sit down right
in front of the prophet to listen: "We want to hear the word of
God from you." That is the implication of their action. But
Ezekiel perceives that inwardly they are not prepared for the total
allegiance to God that authentic biblical religion demands. As
he puts it, they have "set up idols in their hearts."

What does that phrase mean? It could mean two things,
corresponding to the two kinds of idolatry prohibited by the Ten
Commandments. The first commandment forbids the worship
of rival deities. "You shall have no other gods before me" (Ex
20:3). If that kind of idol was what these men were inwardly
reverencing, then it would imply that they were secret devotees
of pagan cults. If that was the case, then their presence at
Ezekiel's sermon was an act of brazen and impertinent hypocrisy.

But there is a second possibility, for the second commandment
forbids the worship of the true God by images. "You shall not make
for yourself an idol" (Ex 20:4). If it was that kind of self-manufac-
tured idol these men had in their hearts, it would imply that they
entertained false ideas about God, derived, maybe, from those false
prophets who prophesied out of their own imagination—ideas
encouraged by the soothing words of the Reverend Whitewash.
This would be a much more subtle offense. For they would then be
unaware that they were idolaters. Their idolatry would consist in
their unwillingness to surrender their preconceived ideas and bow
to the authority of God's revelation through his prophet. In that
sense, it would be an idolatry of the "heart."

Whatever Ezekiel implies, then, by "idolatry in the heart," it surely speaks to us of the way many people pay lip service to evangelical religion today. They are very particular about hearing a good, sound sermon and attending a good, sound church. They revel in being seen in the congregation of a great preacher. But inwardly their heart is not surrendered to God. They have not bowed their will to obey God's law unconditionally; they have not bowed their mind to believe his Word. Every sermon they hear is passed through a mental filter that removes all references to doctrines they find objectionable or to moral commandments they find unacceptable. "Great sermon, Pastor!" they say as they leave, and the pastor is pleased, never realizing that the sermon he preached and the sermon they heard were completely different! They have idols in their hearts and thus put stumbling blocks before their faces. Though there is a large Bible under their arm, for all its penciled notes and carefully underlined texts, it is a pet Bible.

Ezekiel has three things to say to such people. First, there can be no blessing in sitting under biblical ministry while the heart is unyielded to God. Indeed, the opposite is the case.

When any Israelite or any alien living in Israel separates himself from me and sets up idols in his heart and puts a wicked stumbling block before his face and then goes to a prophet to inquire of me, I the LORD will answer him myself. I will set my face against that man and make him an example and a byword. I will cut him off from my people. Then you will know that I am the LORD. (14:7-8)

This is a solemn word. These people were courting disaster if they thought they could maintain this illusion of false spirituality indefinitely. God would expose their hypocrisy one day, to their intense humiliation and embarrassment. It could not go on forever. This is a painful way to learn what God means when he calls himself the Lord.

Second, Ezekiel says, preachers who allow themselves to be

influenced by the presence of such people in their congregation
will share their guilt.

> If the prophet is enticed to utter a prophecy, I the LORD have
> enticed that prophet, and I will stretch out my hand against
> him and destroy him from among my people Israel. They will
> bear their guilt—the prophet will be as guilty as the one who
> consults him. (14:9-10)

What a powerful word this is! It is a great temptation for any
preacher to be compromised by the flattery of influential people
who come to hear his sermons. Evangelical preachers are beginning to be thus flattered these days. It never used to be so. Go
back fifty years, when evangelicals were a despised minority, and
all we got were bricks hurled at us. But now it is quite fashionable
to be evangelical. The evangelical wing of the Church of England
is doing quite nicely, thank you. We even have an evangelical
archbishop now. The danger in that situation is flattery. We
soften the true message of God, tone down the note of repentance. We do not want to put people off. After all, it is very
encouraging that they are coming along to our church.

When that happens, Ezekiel says, the sycophantic prophet
forfeits both his office and his own membership in God's people.
There's a frightening thing for flabby evangelicals to think about!
The purity of God's people depends more than anything else
upon the incorruptibility and integrity of the pulpit. "Then the
people of Israel will no longer stray from me, nor will they defile
themselves anymore with all their sins. They will be my people"
(14:11). The moral and spiritual renewal that revival brings is
always accompanied by the purification of the pulpit.

The third thing that Ezekiel has to say to those who trust in
their evangelical credentials is this: knowing a few godly people
will be no defense in the final judgment.

> Son of man, if a country sins against me by being unfaithful
> and I stretch out my hand against it to cut off its food supply
> and send famine upon it and kill its people and their animals,

even if these three men—Noah, Daniel and Job—were in it,
they could save only themselves by their righteousness, declares the Sovereign LORD. (14:13-14)

Perhaps those elders had sought out Ezekiel because they hoped
to gain some kind of vicarious spirituality through association
with such a person. Come the judgment, it would perhaps be a
point in their favor that they knew Ezekiel. "Lord, I've heard
sermons by Ezekiel. That must be worth a few good marks,
mustn't it?" Many people embrace this kind of superstition.
Worldly and immoral people they may be, but they feel com-
forted at the knowledge that they have a missionary in the family
or that they have attended a service at the church of the famous
and saintly Reverend So-and-So.

But it does not work like that. God says that even if the three
greatest saints of the ancient world—Noah, Daniel and Job—
were numbered among the Israelites, they could pull no strings.
They would save themselves but nobody else. "They could not
save their own sons or daughters" (14:16). What a frightening
thought! The fact that we are related to a true Christian or
worship in a church containing fine Christians will not make a
scrap of difference to our fate when the four horsemen of the
apocalypse ride out in judgment. There are no group tickets to
heaven. The new covenant has nothing to do with the family we
belong to or the fine Christians we count as our friends. As the
old spiritual says, "You got to walk that lonesome valley; you got
to walk there by yourself." No one else can walk it for us.

If we want to be ready for that last day, then, what must we do?
Stop treating the Bible as a pet, says Ezekiel. Stop muzzling its
truth by pretending that the disturbing bits do not apply to you.
Stop covering up your sins with the whitewash of false prophecy.
Stop filtering sermons through your own preconceived ideas.
Stop living as though sitting under biblical ministry were a
substitute for biblical faith and practice. Turn from your evan-
gelical idols and make the Sovereign Lord your God.

Four

The Wounded Lover

E Z E K I E L 16

*E*zekiel 16 is headed in the New International Version "An Allegory of Unfaithful Jerusalem." I find it one of the most moving sections of the whole book. We have already looked at the way Ezekiel uses drama to lend emotional force to his rather somber message of judgment. Another tactic by which he helps his complacent and comfortable audience to engage with his message is allegory. He tells the nation's story in a parabolic way.

The word of the LORD came to me: "Son of man, confront Jerusalem with her detestable practices and say, 'This is what the Sovereign LORD says to Jerusalem: Your ancestry and birth were in the land of the Canaanites; your father was an Amorite and your mother a Hittite. On the day you were born your cord was not cut, nor were you washed with water to make you clean, nor were you rubbed with salt or wrapped in cloths. No one looked on you with pity or had compassion enough to do any of these things for you. Rather, you were thrown out into the open field, for on the day you were born you were despised.

" 'Then I passed by and saw you kicking about in your blood, and as you lay there in your blood I said to you, "Live!" I made you grow like a plant of the field. You grew up and developed and became the most beautiful of jewels. Your breasts were formed and your hair grew, you who were naked and bare.

" 'Later I passed by, and when I looked at you and saw that you were old enough for love, I spread the corner of my garment over you and covered your nakedness. I gave you my solemn oath and entered into a covenant with you, declares the Sovereign LORD, and you became mine.

" 'I bathed you with water and washed the blood from you and put ointments on you. I clothed you with an embroidered dress and put leather sandals on you. I dressed you in fine linen and covered you with costly garments. I adorned you with jewelry: I put bracelets on your arms and a necklace around your neck, and I put a ring on your nose, earrings on your ears and a beautiful crown on your head. So you were adorned with gold and silver; your clothes were of fine linen and costly fabric and embroidered cloth. Your food was fine flour, honey and olive oil. You became very beautiful and rose to be a queen. And your fame spread among the nations on account of your beauty, because the splendor I had given you made your beauty perfect, declares the Sovereign LORD.

" 'But you trusted in your beauty and used your fame to become a prostitute.' " (16:1-15)

Spiritual Adultery

There is nothing that savages the emotions quite like marital breakup. "I know you'll understand," says the terse farewell note on the mantelpiece. But in nine cases out of ten we do not understand and, indeed, why should we? It hurts to be deserted. When we have promised ourselves to someone and invested ourselves emotionally in that person, it is desperately painful to be rejected.

In Britain, the Lord Chancellor attempted to make the divorce legislation less adversarial. But I wonder whether he was sufficiently realistic about the indignation and anger that are legitimately awakened in situations of adultery, unfaithfulness and desertion. The idea that couples can come together and talk things through calmly and quietly before an empathic counselor strikes me as naive. If we make people think that they ought not to feel enraged and humiliated because their partner has walked out on them, or indignant and betrayed because their partner has been unfaithful, and if we make them feel guilty about such emotional responses, we shall create far worse problems of counseling than arose under the adversarial system.

In almost every language *adultery* is a word of shame. Even in the West at the beginning of the twenty-first century, it still carries a social stigma. In ancient Israel the moral reproach that attached to adultery was enormous. In a society based on clan and tribe, the link between social stability and the inviolability of the marriage bond was evident to all. Everybody sensed that the consequences of adultery could not be confined to just one family. The whole social order was threatened. And that, no doubt, is one of the reasons Moses placed it on the list of capital crimes. In the mind of a Jew, it was a terribly shameful thing to accuse someone of adultery.

Perhaps that helps us to understand the incident when some Jews brought to Jesus the woman caught in the act of adultery (Jn 8:1-11). We read that Jesus bent down and wrote with his finger in the dust. Some have suggested that he wrote a list of the sins of the accusers, to expose their hypocrisy. But I have often wondered whether he was not turning his face away in sheer embarrassment at the salacious delight these people were taking in this woman's wanton behavior. Their parading this matter in public was vulgar. They clearly did not appreciate the shamefulness of sin; they simply sought an opportunity to score a debating point or two over Jesus. Might it be that their indelicacy so offended the sensitivity of God's Son as to cause him to blush and turn away, and to doodle for a few moments in order to recover himself? Certainly adultery is a shocking and disgusting thing to God, as disgraceful and reprehensible a crime as murder. It is not something that even he speaks of calmly and without emotion.

All this makes it more remarkable that adultery is precisely the crime with which Ezekiel charges the people of Jerusalem in this chapter. "You adulterous wife!" he cries. "You prefer strangers to your own husband!" (16:32). No more emotive words could have been chosen. The prophet's language is quite deliberately intended to shock and to embarrass. Israel's idolatry, he says, is not something God views with the detached objectivity of a conciliation counselor appointed by a court of law. He feels passionately about this. Why? Because God is not some distant deity to his people. He is their husband. The covenant that binds him to them is no loose agreement; it is a marriage vow. So when Israel rejects God's standards, it is spiritual adultery, says the prophet.

Ezekiel develops this analogy at length in this chapter. The allegory is one of three extended metaphors that he inserts at this point in his prophecy, the other two being the allegory of the vine (chapter 15) and the allegory of the two eagles (chapter 17). In different ways all of them give expression to God's bitter disappointment with Jerusalem, but there is no doubt that this central allegory of the unfaithful wife is by far the most emotive.

The Patient Lover

"Later I passed by, and when I looked at you and saw that you were old enough for love, I spread the corner of my garment over you and covered your nakedness" (16:8). That is a classic Hebrew way of expressing marriage. There is a tenderness and pathos in these verses as God, so to speak, looks back on his experience of young love. He scans the centuries to recall how he had first encountered Israel. She was an illegitimate child of

pagan parents, he said, in the land of the Canaanites. Her
father was an Amorite and her mother a Hittite. She was a
deprived child born in ignorance and filth: "On the day you
were born your cord was not cut, nor were you washed with
water to make you clean, nor were you rubbed with salt or
wrapped in cloths." She was an unwanted child, destined to
die of exposure: "No one looked on you with pity or had
compassion enough to do any of these things for you. Rather,
you were thrown out into the open field." God recalls how he
took this unlovable infant, even as she lay in the pool of her
own placental remains, and adopted her as his own. "I passed
by and saw you kicking about in your blood, and as you lay
there in your blood I said to you, 'Live!'" (16:4-6).

As in a fairy story, Israel's rags turned to riches as she grew
through childhood and into adolescence. Her original ugli-
ness is forgotten, and, says the allegory, an unexpected beauty
is revealed. "You grew up and developed and became the most
beautiful of jewels" (16:7). He whose pity had once moved him
to adopt her as his daughter now embraces her afresh as his
bride: "I spread the corner of my garment over you . . . I gave
you my solemn oath and entered into a covenant with you . . .
and you became mine" (16:8). With that change, his generosity
toward this girl overflows with new and inexhaustible extrava-
gance: "I bathed you with water and washed the blood from you
and put ointments on you" (16:9). What a beautiful picture of
the way God showered prosperity on Israel in the early days,
after the sealing of the Mosaic covenant at Sinai, up to the
glorious monarchies of David and Solomon! From first to last,
says the prophet, it has been the story of God's loving initiative.
Now God looks back on those days with the nostalgia of a
middle-aged family man who comes across his wedding photos
in the attic. What precious things memories are in a successful
marriage! But what a tragic source of heartbreak those same
memories become when the marriage drifts onto the rocks.

The Jilted Lover

A man once brought me his wedding photos and wept over them. Regrettably, that is what happened in Israel's case. Patient, electing love gave way to the wounded heart of a jilted lover. "But you trusted in your beauty and used your fame to become a prostitute. You lavished your favors on anyone who passed by and your beauty became his" (16:15).

Christian theologians of the past have sometimes spoken of the impassibility of God, the belief that God cannot suffer. I have problems with the idea. It seems to me far more Greek than Christian. The god of the Stoics certainly could not suffer. The Stoic god was an emotionally petrified deity impervious to the surging passions of human beings. Isolated in the island of his own self-sufficiency, he needed nobody. Those who believed in such a god sought to copy his detached indifference to pain.

But the Stoic god is completely unlike the God of the Bible. What is the cross of Calvary if not a terrifying confirmation of the agony that tears the heart of God because of his people's sin? And what is Ezekiel portraying to us here if not the plaintive cry of suffering born of unrequited love? Surely we can sense the injury God feels in Israel's rejection of him in this story. "You lavished your favors on anyone who passed by," he says, "and your beauty became his. You took some of your garments to make gaudy high places, where you carried on your prostitution. Such things should not happen, nor should they ever occur" (16:15-16). Hear the indignation in his voice. He is referring, of course, to the idolatry with which Israel became embroiled. He speaks of how the wealth with which he had enriched the nation was used to build shrines for foreign deities. "You took your embroidered clothes to put on [the idols], and you offered my oil and incense before them. Also the food I provided for you—the fine flour, olive oil and honey I gave you to eat—you offered as fragrant incense before them" (16:18-19). The land of milk and honey, then, was offered in sacrifice on pagan altars.

But that was not the worst. "You took your sons and daughters whom you bore to me and sacrificed them as food to the idols. Was your prostitution not enough? You slaughtered my children and sacrificed them to the idols" (16:20-21). Child sacrifice was a well-established part of the worship of Moloch. Though Moses explicitly prohibited it, there are early references to the practice in the period of the Israelite monarchy and ironically it was, as Ezekiel implies, in the days of the nation's greatest economic prosperity that this cult first became firmly established in Jerusalem. Solomon himself was the first king to build a sanctuary to Moloch, no doubt to satisfy the whim of his Ammonite wives, for whom Moloch was a national patron.

Notice how God describes what they have done in this respect. "You slaughtered my children," he says. Could this accusation have some relevance to the current debate about abortion? We hear a lot about the rights of the mother and the rights of the unborn child, but I wonder whether Christians should not also be concerned about *God's* rights over infant life. These are his children we are slaughtering. It seems the ingratitude of it all—even more than the inhumanity—stings the heart of God: "In all your detestable practices and your prostitution you did not remember the days of your youth, when you were naked and bare, kicking about in your blood" (16:22).

The sorry tale of spiritual degeneracy winds on as Israel's infatuation with these foreign gods becomes obsessive. She sets up crude pagan symbols in public places in the city: "At the head of every street you built your lofty shrines and degraded your beauty, offering your body with increasing promiscuity to anyone who passed by" (16:25). Squares and street corners, then, were saturated with this spiritual wantonness. "Offering your body" is what the NIV says. The Hebrew is cruder: "You open your legs to anyone." She embraces even the gods of those cruel nations that ought to have been her sworn enemies: "the Egyptians, your lustful neighbors" (16:26), the Assyrians and the Philistines

(16:27-28), and the Babylonians (16:29). But with all this, he says, "you were not satisfied" (16:29). Even pagans, such as the Philistines, were outraged by the enthusiasm with which Israel jeopardized her cultural distinctiveness. The heathen nations were more faithful to their nonexistent divinities than Israel to the Lord.

Initially, no doubt, these flirtations were politically motivated. The presence of a foreign temple in the capital in those early days of the monarchy often indicated a military alliance, much as American bases in Europe indicate commitment to NATO. One could argue that Israel was forced into such alliances during the period of the monarchy and that allowances should be made for this. But Israel's appetite for idolatry, Ezekiel insists, went far beyond the requirements of political expediency. She no longer asked what she would gain from her pagan sugar daddies; she was prepared to pay for the privilege of her illicit affairs. An inverted prostitute! She sought new gods like an animal in heat, he says. Like a spiritual nymphomaniac, she knew no shame.

> How weak-willed you are . . . when you do all these things, acting like a brazen prostitute! When you built your mounds at the head of every street and made your lofty shrines in every public square, you were unlike a prostitute, because you scorned payment. . . .
>
> Every prostitute receives a fee, but you give gifts to all your lovers, bribing them to come to you from everywhere for your illicit favors. So in your prostitution you are the opposite of others; no one runs after you for your favors. You are the very opposite, for you give payment and none is given to you. (16:30-31, 33-34)

The imagery is shocking, and it is meant to make us squirm with embarrassment. (And the Hebrew is less restrained than the English translation!) But it is only by such language that the prophet can communicate to us just how deeply outraged is the heart of God by this apostasy among his people. It is spiritual adultery, nothing less. His chosen bride has made a cuckold of him, and he cannot take such unfaithfulness lightly or sentimentally. His tears mingle with his rage.

The Jealous Lover

Therefore, you prostitute, hear the word of the LORD! This is what the Sovereign LORD says: Because you poured out your wealth and exposed your nakedness in your promiscuity with your lovers, and because of all your detestable idols, and because you gave them your children's blood, therefore I am going to gather all your lovers, with whom you found pleasure, those you loved as well as those you hated. I will gather them against you from all around and will strip you in front of them, and they will see all your nakedness. (16:35-37)

It is a grave mistake to underestimate the significance of those words in the second commandment, "I, the LORD your God, am a jealous God" (Ex 20:5). We think of jealousy as a vice, but that is because we habitually confuse it with covetousness. It is one thing to desire something that belongs to somebody else: that is envy or covetousness, and that is a sin. It is another thing altogether to guard with possessive zeal that which is rightfully and exclusively one's own: that is jealousy. If someone steals my wallet, I am angry, and rightly so. I am jealous of my wallet; it is mine. Similarly, in biblical ethics, if someone steals my wife, I am angry, and rightly so, because I am jealous over my wife: she is mine too. Although earlier English law was scandalous in the way that it sometimes treated a wife as a chattel, the biblical truth is that a husband has property in his wife and a wife has property in her husband—they belong to each other. That is the significance of the possessive pronouns in this allegory. "You became mine," says God.

The glorification of communal ownership in our day threatens this fundamental moral truth. A basic flaw in Marxist ethics is that by denying private property it is incapable of distinguishing covetousness from jealousy. It is no surprise, therefore, that a Marxist ethic can never really understand the nature and power of marital affection. God suffers no such blind spot. He is a jealous husband and not embarrassed to call himself such. Moreover, he will prosecute for any breach of his property rights. "I will sentence you to the punishment of women who commit adultery," he says (16:38). Ironically, the agents of God's judgment are going to be the very nations whose gods Israel has sported with: "I will hand you over to your lovers, and they will tear down your mounds and destroy your lofty shrines. They will strip you of your clothes and take your fine jewelry and leave you naked and bare" (16:39).

She will be publicly humiliated. These are the penalties demanded, and not until they are executed will God's fury abate.

I think this passage can rightly be applied to Britain too, because of the spiritual privilege our nation has received over nearly two thousand years of Christian history. We are not a covenant nation in the sense Israel was, but we are a hugely blessed nation. God has been very good to this nation, out of proportion to our deserts. Yet at the beginning of the twenty-first century, we find Britain, and the West generally, surrendering to exactly the kind of religious pluralism as Israel. We are abandoning the faith of our forebears. The economic problems we complain of so much—inflation, high interest rates, the trade deficit—are all the direct result of our insatiable demand for the immediate gratification of our materialistic greed. Similarly, the social problems that distress us so much—the crime rate, child abuse, violence among soccer fans, AIDS and so many more—are the direct result of collectively repudiating the law of God which we have known for centuries but which we have spurned in favor of selfishness and lust. There is surely, then, a sense in which God's word of judgment against Jerusalem is a word also to us. A people who have been as blessed as we have can expect only the judgment of God if we are ungrateful for those privileges and abuse them.

This seems to me a very powerful lesson for the church in our day too. We often think of judgment as something that falls on the heathen, upon atheists, upon criminals, upon non-Christians. But Ezekiel's message is first and foremost a message to Jerusalem, to the visible church. God had given her the opportunity to be the envy of the world. He had showered his grace upon her, and she had turned her back on him. God demands much of those to whom much is given. If there is one thing more frightening than to fall into the hands of the living God (Heb 10:31), it is to fall out of his hands.

Is God pleased with the church in lands with a Christian heritage? Are we the kind of people he is likely to revive and bless? It seems to me that the Western church is hopelessly compromised by the spirit of the age. It is a church that demands healing far more than it is prepared to endure suffering; a church that wants prosperity far more than it is ready to face adversity; a church that is much more interested in status symbols than in stigmata; a church that in numerous ways simply echoes the idolatrous practices of the world around.

Christianity is always a rescue religion. It is about saving people. Sometimes the church itself needs to hear that message of rescue as much as the world does.

Some might charge that to preach judgment is to stoop to the unscrupulous tactics of intimidation. C. S. Lewis gave a wise reply to this when he said that the remarkable thing is that God will accept sinners even when they come to him as nothing better than frightened people clutching at straws. It is hardly complimentary to treat God as simply an alternative to judgment! If God were proud, he would not accept us on such terms. The glorious and gracious thing about this humble God the Bible reveals to us is that he is always willing to receive his people back even on the basis of repentance prompted by no higher motive than fear. He is willing to accept people who would never come to him at all if the flames of hell were not scorching their heels.

"Flee from the coming wrath," John the Baptist told the visible church of his day (Mt 3:7). Jonathan Edwards told the nominal believers in New England that there would be no revival unless the word of judgment were heard first, for there can be no salvation unless people know that they are in danger. Only when they have heard that disturbing truth does Ezekiel begin to apply the healing balm of grace.

The Constant Lover

> This is what the Sovereign LORD says: I will deal with you as you deserve, because you have despised my oath by breaking the covenant. Yet I will remember the covenant I made with you in the days of your youth, and I will establish an everlasting covenant with you. (16:59-60)

In these final verses Ezekiel introduces a new element into the allegory, though it is closely related to what has gone before. Israel was first pictured as a foundling child who grew up, became a wife and then turned to prostitution—in spite of the lavish care of her adoptive parent and loving husband. Now, in 16:45-47, her true mother appears on the scene, and Israel joins the family brothel. Mother and daughters all engage in a lecherous conspiracy. Ezekiel is not afraid to mention the other women in the house:

> You are a true daughter of your mother, who despised her husband and her children; and you are a true sister of your sisters, who despised their husbands and their children. Your mother was a Hittite and your father an Amorite. Your older sister was Samaria, who lived to the north of you with her daughters; and your younger sister, who lived to the south of you with her daughters, was Sodom. (16:45-46)

It is hard to imagine how infuriating it would be to Jewish nationalists, of whom there were many in exile at this time, to be reminded of their ethnic link with other Semitic peoples in the Middle East whom they had always regarded as their racial

inferiors. The suggestion of kinship with Sodom was rank insult.
But Ezekiel is adamant. Among all these brazen hussies, he says,
Israel is by far the most debauched.

> You not only walked in their ways and copied their detestable
> practices, but in all your ways you soon became more depraved
> than they. As surely as I live, declares the Sovereign LORD, your
> sister Sodom and her daughters never did what you and your
> daughters have done. (16:47-48)

Initially, then, it seems that Ezekiel, by invoking this supplemen-
tary allegory, is simply seeking to underline the grossness of
Israel's spiritual failure which is already portrayed in the first half
of the chapter. But it soon becomes clear that there is more to it
than that.

> Samaria did not commit half the sins you did. You have done
> more detestable things than they, and have made your sisters
> seem righteous by all these things you have done. Bear your
> disgrace, for you have furnished some justification for your
> sisters. Because your sins were more vile than theirs, they
> appear more righteous than you. So then, be ashamed and
> bear your disgrace, for you have made your sisters appear
> righteous.
>
> However, I will restore the fortunes of Sodom and her
> daughters and of Samaria and her daughters, and your for-
> tunes along with them, so that you may bear your disgrace and
> be ashamed of all you have done in giving them comfort.
> (16:51-54)

This is a most remarkable passage. God is saying that one of the
ways he intends to shame Israel for her bad behavior is by
restoring her in company with the Gentile nations she once
despised. This will be humiliating for Israel, he says. "You would
not even mention your sister Sodom in the day of your pride"
(16:56). Israel used to think herself superior and would be
grossly offended to have her name linked with Sodom. But the
days are coming, says Ezekiel, when that chauvinistic pride will

be broken, and the Jews will have to acknowledge that they belong to the same family of sin as Sodom and Samaria. God will treat them all identically. There will be no more favoritism.

> I will deal with you as you deserve, because you have despised my oath by breaking the covenant. Yet I will remember the covenant I made with you in the days of your youth, and I will establish an everlasting covenant with you. Then you will remember your ways and be ashamed when you receive your sisters, both those who are older than you and those who are younger. I will give them to you as daughters, but not on the basis of my covenant with you. So I will establish my covenant with you, and you will know that I am the LORD. Then, when I make atonement for you for all you have done, you will remember and be ashamed and never again open your mouth because of your humiliation, declares the Sovereign LORD. (16:59-63)

What remarkable insight from God's prophet! Though Israel may prove false to her marriage vow, he says, God cannot abandon his promise so lightly. He could justly divorce Israel, but he still feels bound by his vow to remain faithful to her in spite of all her sin. Since Israel cannot commend herself to God on the ground of her righteousness, this means that his dealings with her have to be on the grounds of yet more grace. He himself must make atonement for her sins. But if God offers forgiveness to Israel, whom he could justly reject, how can he refuse it to those others in the fallen race of humanity who have sinned less wantonly than Israel has, in spite of the fact that they had no covenantal obligations to keep?

Thus Ezekiel, in his prophetic wrestling with this problem, is led to the outstanding conclusion that God will one day reconfirm that covenant relationship with his people, but it will no longer be an exclusive arrangement with Israel. The Jews will have to accept their Gentile neighbors as sisters, as cobeneficiaries of a new and everlasting covenant in which there will be no more distinctions on the basis of race. That would be part of Israel's penalty and national humiliation, because of her failure to discharge the responsibilities that went with the old covenant.

This fascinating prophetic anticipation of the gospel of Jesus Christ sheds light on one of the most difficult chapters in the whole of the New Testament: Romans 11.

> I ask then [says the apostle]: Did God reject his people? By no means! I am an Israelite myself. . . . Did they stumble so as to fall beyond recovery? Not at all! Rather, because of [Israel's] transgression, salvation has come to the Gentiles to make Israel envious. (Rom 11:1, 11)

What did Paul have in mind, if not Ezekiel 16?

> God's gifts and his call are irrevocable. Just as you [Gentiles] who were at one time disobedient to God have now received mercy as a result of their disobedience, so they too have now become disobedient in order that they too may receive mercy as a result of God's mercy to you. For God has bound everyone over to disobedience so that he may have mercy on them all. (Rom 11:29-32)

The strange strategy of God in the old covenant, then, was to allow Israel to prostitute herself in this flagrant way so that he might win the whole world by an act of grace. The fact that Israel turned out no better than her pagan relations, in spite of all the special privileges heaped upon her, had the effect of widening the scope of God's forgiveness to embrace men and women of every race and religious background without discrimination. Thus Israel's transgression means "riches for the Gentiles," says Paul (Rom 11:12).

God and His People Today

Here, then, we have an allegory of God the patient lover, who chose his people when they were far from lovely in his eyes; God the jilted lover, whose heart is savaged because his people are sinful; God the jealous lover, whose anger is part of his love; and

God the constant lover, who deals with his people in reconciling grace. How are we to apply all this to our hearts and situation today?

First, this allegory points out in unmistakable terms what a serious matter sin is in the life of God's people. "You became very beautiful and rose to be a queen. And your fame spread among the nations . . . because the splendor I had given you made your beauty perfect" (16:13-14).

What love and tenderness there is in God's evaluation of his people! Biblical religion is not just a matter of how we feel toward God, but also of how he feels toward us. We are as precious to him as a wife to her husband. Dare we say it, he is emotionally bound up with us. He loves the church and gave himself for her. So when we fail to honor him, when we put other things at the center of our affections rather than give him first place, he does not feel mildly irritated. He experiences all the passion of a wounded husband, the hurt and rage of a victim of adultery. Perhaps, then, we need to fear sin more. God is not a heavenly policeman, nabbing people when they break an external law. The moral law is the law of his own holy character. When we break his commandments, we hurt him. Nor is God an academic theologian working out some detached belief system, for the doctrines of the Bible are the truths of his own divine nature. When we worship idols, we hurt him. Sin is not something God can describe neutrally and objectively, like a surgeon clinically commenting on the presence of a cancer. It is a personal offense. It seems to me that we are losing touch today with this understanding of what sin is.

We need to relate this as much to the theological scene as to the moral scene in our society. Pluralism has swept in, and elements of Buddhism, Marxism, Hinduism and all sorts of other beliefs are being mixed into the potpourri of Christo-mysticism. In the sophisticated atmosphere of the university or the lecture hall, this eclectic policy may seem commendably tolerant and ecumenical. But it was just such a syncretistic attitude that Israel was demonstrating toward the religions of its contemporary world. Ezekiel did not call that policy enlightened scholarship; he called it spiritual prostitution. That, he says, is how God sees these flirtations with nonbiblical ideas within the church. He does not call it theologically liberal; he calls it theologically licentious. Some scholars seem to feel that because of their position as creative researchers they must be allowed room for speculation and experiment. God's response is to challenge them: "How weak-willed you are" (16:30). Sin in the life of God's people is serious, and nothing can be more serious than this theological sin that dabbles in idolatrous ideas and tries to incorporate them into the religion of God's people. God will not stand idly by and watch his bride prostituting herself in that way. There must be judgment on a church that allows undisciplined error to perpetuate itself within its midst. There has to be. If God feels as intensely as this about it, he will surely do something to put matters right.

The second point we can draw from Ezekiel's picture is the spiritual ruin that backsliding brings upon an individual Christian's relationship with God. "Because you did not remember the days of your youth but enraged me with all these things, I will surely bring down on your head what you have done, declares the Sovereign LORD" (16:43).

Sometimes it worries me to remember the sort of Christian I was when first converted. In some ways I was a much keener and more zealous Christian then than I am now. Is not this the experience of many? We remember how enthusiastic we were, how devoted, how much time we spent in prayer and Bible study, how concerned we were to know God's will and obey it. We were more naive and less theologically sophisticated, but there was a passion there then. We remember the days of our spiritual youth, as it were, when God called us graciously to himself and we first experienced the delight of being loved by him. How does God remember those days now? Does he remember them with the sweetness and joy of a husband whose marriage has deepened over the years or with the bitterness and disappointment of a man whose wife has been unfaithful to him? It is a sobering question.

A backsliding Christian is always a miserable person, just as apostate Israel was a miserable nation. No one is more miserable than a backsliding Christian. Nothing is more miserable, I think, than an apostate church. Sinners can enjoy themselves, at least for a while; but the person who really belongs to Christ and forsakes him is like a fish out of water. God will not allow such people to enjoy their sin for very long. The Spirit he has placed within us grieves over us. Guilt burns our conscience and a blush rises to our face whenever someone says, "Let's pray." The spiritual dissatisfaction gnaws at hearts. It is a terrible thing to have tasted the joy of a relationship with God and then to have lost it. No one is sadder or lonelier than a spiritual divorcée. Yet backsliding is common today under pressure from the worldliness of our age.

Third, we can and should take comfort from the emphasis in this passage on the unshakable faithfulness of God to his covenant. "I will remember the covenant I made with you in the days of your youth" (16:60). God will chasten his true people for their sin, but if we are bought with the blood of Christ he can never damn us for it. He will humiliate his church, maybe, demolishing our pride and numbering us with the moral scum of the world. Yet this scum he is determined to save! Sometimes I think that the church in our day has walked in the streets of spiritual prostitution in a way not unlike Israel in Ezekiel's day, careless of the suffering that we have added to Christ's agony on the cross. The emptiness of soul that has afflicted the Western church in recent years is part of the price we pay for that. Many of us in our individual lives share that same spiritual emptiness. But we can be encouraged that God will take us back, for his grace is inexhaustible.

I once counseled a couple who went through a period of estrangement as a result of the unfaithfulness of one partner. Marvelously, they were brought back together again. "You know," the wife said to me, "when our marriage was breaking up it was sheer hell, but making up again has been like a second honeymoon." Maybe there is a spiritual corollary to that. Perhaps we need a second honeymoon with God. His arms are wide open if so.

Perhaps too there is a word of pastoral advice here for those who are passing through marital crises. I sometimes find that it helps and encourages people in that situation to grasp the idea that even though they are experiencing great pain, they are uniquely placed to engage emotionally with the passion of Christ. Used positively, that kind of marital suffering can be turned into something immensely enriching spiritually. It takes us up into the heart of God in a way few other experiences of life can. We understand the suffering of the cross far better when we ourselves know the pain of rejection.

The Necessity of Compassion

The final implication I want to draw out of this passage is this: all the time we are standing for truth and proclaiming God's judgment, we must not lose the quality of compassion. Some people love a good argument. They are in their element writing defamatory letters to the press and indignant pamphlets. Certain branches of evangelical Christianity seem to attract that type of dogmatic authoritarianism. There are people in the church who love to denounce error, heresy, apostasy and permissiveness. Their publications are full of capital letters, exclamation marks, and references to the whore of Babylon, the antichrist and so on. Very often their concern is right. Why then do I feel uncomfortable about the apocalyptic anathemas they heap upon the rest of the world? Because they seem to be enjoying it so much. The false prophets arouse their aggressive instincts. They leap on controversy with cruel delight. That does not seem to me to be the response of people who are trying to echo, in their own emotional reaction, the heart of God. Yes, there is anger in God's heart, but there is also pain and a great desire for reconciliation.

Israel broke God's heart. They had hurt him. Ezekiel did not enjoy being in this situation. He did not want to be a controversialist. The false prophets were a source of deep distress to him. We should beware, then, of mistaking natural belligerence for spiritual zeal. If there is no compassion in our hearts when we do battle for God's truth, I wonder if we really are speaking for this divine lover of Ezekiel 16. It is said that when the great preacher George Whitefield spoke of judgment, he did so with tears. "The Lord's servant must not quarrel; instead, he must be kind to everyone," says the apostle. "Those who oppose him he must gently instruct" (2 Tim 2:24-25).

Our Savior himself stood for truth. "For this reason I was born," he told Pilate, "to testify to the truth" (Jn 18:37). But he stood for that truth not with a sword in his hand but with a cross on his back. If we would stand for truth, then, let us do so with his humility and compassion.

Five

Truth & Tolerance

DANIEL 1

G. K. Chesterton once wrote that when people stop believing in the truth, they do not believe in nothing; they believe in anything. That insightful comment sums up, I think, the state of Western society today. People in the 1990s have indeed stopped believing in the truth. The concept of a body of ideas or teaching that claims universal and unconditional acceptance by virtue of its absolute veracity has gone out of fashion. The result is as Chesterton predicted: not skepticism but gullibility. We are assailed by an assortment of religions and philosophies, all given exposure on prime-time television and all represented by militant pressure groups in the community. People become increasingly bewildered. It does not seem possible, or even polite, to express either certainty or conviction on religious issues anymore. We do not believe in nothing; we believe in anything and everything.

In *The Heretical Imperative*, sociologist Peter Berger describes the situation as living in a supermarket of worldviews. When we have a headache, we can choose from a variety of painkillers in the supermarket. In the same way, he says, we can now choose from a host of understandings of the world in which we live.

As with painkillers, each brand has its own advertisers assuring us that it is the best, but the suspicion grows in the mind of the weary consumer that in fact there is nothing to choose between them. People suspect that George Bernard Shaw was right when he said that there is only one religion in the world but a hundred versions of it.

The defense most commonly brought in support of this pluralist mindset is that it is essential to democracy. Karl Popper, in *The Open Society and Its Enemies,* argues cogently that the belief that one has *the* truth is always implicitly totalitarian. The only safely democratic state of mind, he says, is to adopt an attitude of permanent uncertainty about all issues of ideology and worldview, because it is a small step from the certainty that says, "I am sure," to the tyranny that says, "Therefore I must be obeyed."

At the level of the ordinary person, Popper's arguments come down to that little word that one hears so often: *tolerance.* Living, as we do, with Hindu temples, Muslim mosques and Christian churches side by side on Main Street, we cannot be exclusivist about religion anymore. In the marketplace of ideas, monopolies cannot be allowed; that would only cause trouble. Every religious option has to be as socially acceptable as every other or conflict will ensue. Tolerance is the name of the game. The time has passed when Christians could say with the clergyman in Henry Fielding's *Tom Jones,* "When I mention religion, I mean the Christian religion; and not only the Christian religion, but the Protestant religion, and not only the Protestant religion but the Church of England." Now when we mention *religion,* the word embraces every variety of spirituality under the sun!

This is where New Age ideas are proving so attractive to the modern mood. According to New Age thought, it is not the content of your belief that matters but the personal enrichment you discover by believing it. So believe anything or everything if you like. Eastern mysticism has been teaching this for centuries. It can accommodate just about any creed on its religious smorgasbord, and so it represents the ideal platform on which to build a hypertolerant, multifaith, pluralist society.

What people fail to realize when they bandy about this emotive word *tolerance* is that the nature of tolerance changes in a pluralist society like ours. At the end of the seventeenth century, when the Act of Toleration was passed in Britain, *toleration* referred to a virtue born out of confidence in the ability of the truth to vindicate itself without instruments of state oppression. But at the dawn of the twenty-first century we now question whether the truth lies anywhere, or whether indeed the very word *truth* has any meaning at all. And the irony of that is that New Age eclecticism comes to represent not tolerance at all, but in fact a resurgence of the oldest and least liberal form of society known to humanity, namely paganism. Nineteenth-century prime minister William Ewart Gladstone, in words that are strangely prophetic, warned that if we abandon the truth claims of Christianity and the way in which it anchors religious truth in objective history and objective fact, and turn to the old pluralist syncretism of the Roman Empire, then we shall return also to the intolerance of Rome. For the only thing that cannot be tolerated in such a society is a group of people who say they have the truth. Already we are beginning to see evidence that Christians are finding it hard to survive in certain professions because of the absolutism they encounter when they insist that there are ethical and creedal norms which they cannot surrender.

The end result of secularization, then, is not a neutral world in which all can freely pursue their chosen purposes, but a pagan world in which occultism and superstition of a thousand kinds are given free rein in a new pantheon, and the only faith that will not be tolerated is faith in a Jesus who makes exclusive truth claims.

All of this makes Daniel a hero for today. He too found himself in a pagan society, a society that was hostile to his faith and that was determined to undermine it by state-sponsored idolatries of various kinds. The story of how Daniel survived as a believer is one of the most vivid narratives the Bible contains, and it is a story we need to hear again on the edge of the twenty-first century, for the church is going to need such heroes again.

In this chapter and the next four, we shall look at the way Daniel illustrates Christian heroism in the face of paganism. How do we know when to put our foot down in a pagan society that undermines us at every turn? Daniel gives us some important guidelines on that. How can we be salt in the world and yet preserve our saltiness? How can we be "the light of the world" rather than "a lamp . . . under a bowl" (Mt 5:14-15)? Daniel shows us beautifully how to hold these things in tension—how to be in the world but not of it (Jn 17:16).

Daniel's First Stand

Daniel 1 is a key chapter (though less dramatic than later ones) because it shows us a young man learning to take his stand. The issue was really quite minor, but in the long run it probably had far-reaching consequences in his personal life.

> The king ordered Ashpenaz, chief of his court officials, to bring in some of the Israelites from the royal family and the nobility— young men without any physical defect, handsome, showing aptitude for every kind of learning, well informed, quick to understand, and qualified to serve in the king's palace. He was to teach them the language and literature of the Babylonians. The king assigned them a daily amount of food and wine from the king's table. They were to be trained for three years, and after that they were to enter the king's service.
>
> Among these were some from Judah: Daniel . . . (1:3-6)

This generous educational program that Nebuchadnezzar pro- vided for selected young aristocrats was clearly politically motivated. It was a maneuver designed to assimilate them into Babylonian culture and thus turn potential rebels into compliant vassals. An intensive degree course in Chaldean liberal arts at the University of Babylon would surely be enough to sever the Jewish roots of these impressionable youngsters irreversibly. *Why,* he thought, *we may even turn these gauche and recalcitrant country bumpkins from Jerusalem into candidates for the Royal Diplomatic Corps. By the end of the course they will be so Babylonian they won't even remember their Hebrew names. We'll make sure of that.* So they gave Daniel the name Belteshazzar.

It was an ingenious scheme. If Ashpenaz was right about the results of their IQ tests, Daniel and his friends would not be able to resist the intellectual stimulation and challenge of so much learning: new languages to learn, new books to read, new subjects to study that had never been heard of in Jerusalem, such as science and mathematics and astronomy. It must have seemed irresistibly intoxicating. The feast of learning was made all the more palatable, of course, by the quality of the college meals! For every day these favored young men dined at high table with food brought straight from the emperor's own kitchens.

Unexpectedly, that is the issue on which Daniel puts his foot down: "But Daniel resolved not to defile himself with the royal food and wine" (1:8). Why? Why did Daniel take this obstreperous line? After all, we do not read that he made any complaint about his new Babylonian name. He certainly did not boycott lectures at his new Babylonian university. On the contrary, we are told that at his oral examination before the emperor he and his three friends graduated summa cum laude. So there is no evidence of blank examination papers or anti-Babylonian demonstrations. They were model students. If Daniel was willing to cooperate with so much of the cultural assimilation program to which he and his friends were being subjected, why object to the food?

Some answer that it must have been because of some ritual taboo. Jewish law did, of course, lay down certain dietary regulations. Did Daniel refuse to eat because the food was not kosher? That seems doubtful, for we read that he objected to the wine as much as to the meat, and there was no ceremonial prohibition on alcohol in the law of Moses. Yet clearly Daniel's reluctance to eat the emperor's food was religious in origin, because the writer uses the word *defile* (1:8). This word strongly implies that he saw the issue as one of moral or spiritual pollution. It was not just that he was vegetarian or that he had trouble adjusting to a foreign diet. This was an issue of religious conscience for him. To eat of the king's food would have been, for Daniel, to compromise his personal holiness in some way.

But again we ask, why? Some have suggested that Daniel's scruples in this matter were due to the fact that the emperor's food would have been consecrated to idols before it was served. This may have been true, but the text makes no mention of it, and in fact it is unlikely that the vegetables Daniel was offered instead were any less contaminated by pagan rituals. In any case, how could he have been sure?

The only conclusion we can safely draw is that Daniel judged this sharing in the king's table to be one step further than he was prepared to go in accommodating himself as a Jew to his new situation in a pagan world. As a believer, surrounded by this pagan pantheon of religions that Babylonia offered, he felt he had to draw a line somewhere, and this was where he decided to draw it. Perhaps he reasoned that eating with someone, especially in the ancient world, was a sign of friendship. In a diplomatic context, eating together often implied a political alliance. But Daniel was a member of a nation that was bound by exclusive covenant to Yahweh, the only God. No other loyalty could ever be permitted to usurp the priority of that relationship in Daniel's life. He was determined on that. He seems to have felt that eating food from the king's table, even if the king was not personally present, threatened that loyalty to an unacceptable degree. It created, perhaps, a feeling of intimacy between him and his pagan master that was too close for comfort.

Wasn't Daniel being excessively sensitive and scrupulous on this point? Would eating from the king's table really have done any spiritual harm to him and his friends? Doesn't Jesus say that it is not the food that goes into the mouth that makes one unclean but the things that come from the heart (Mt 15:10-20)? Surely in that case it was up to Daniel whether he allowed himself to be defiled by this Babylonian banquet or not. Was it not possible for him to enjoy the good food and still retain an uncompromising devotion to God? In theory, perhaps it was. But it seems that Daniel found it impossible in practice, at least for him personally. He felt the need to draw a line somewhere or else be swept into wholesale denial of his Jewish origins. Notice the way the writer puts it: "Daniel resolved not to defile himself." This was a personal decision. Literally, "he purposed in his heart." I think the Hebrew phrase suggests an inner wrestling with conscience that resulted in personal determination to make a stand of principle on the matter.

I believe there may have been three factors influencing his mind as he engaged in that inner struggle. First, he may have felt the need to dissociate himself from the emperor as a testimony to his Babylonian tutors. He may have believed this was a gesture of witness, as if he were saying, "I may be acquiescing in your educational program, but don't you run away with the idea that I'm abandoning my Jewish roots. The emperor can't bribe me into becoming one of his stooges. I have no choice but to be his servant, but I'll never volunteer to become his ally."

Second, maybe he felt that his action was necessary to boost the morale of his fellow students. He does seem to have had some leadership role amongst his peers, Shadrach, Meshach and Abednego. He may have wanted to convey to them the idea that although they were Nebuchadnezzar's guinea pigs in this educational crash course, they did not have to be his puppy dogs, begging tidbits from their master's table. They could show these

Babylonians that they intended to retain that Jewish dignity and independence by a little student protest.

My feeling, however, is that primarily Daniel felt this move was necessary *personally*, as an affirmation of his own spiritual commitment, and to prevent the corruption of his own heart in this alien situation. Perhaps there was nothing technically sinful about eating the king's food, but, for Daniel, a believer needing to sustain and practice a biblical faith in a pagan environment, it was one step too far, one concession too many. He knew himself well enough to realize that he was not immune to the enticements of Babylonian culture: the fascination of occultism and magic which Babylonian learning excelled in; the opportunity for political ambition which his training would equip him for; the seduction of pagan women, of whom no doubt the Babylonian court possessed many. He was surrounded daily by dozens of temptations to apostasy, temptations to which he knew he was not impervious.

If Daniel was to remain true to God in the face of this assault on his spirituality, it would require immense self-discipline. He simply could not allow himself to be softened up by the king's food. Why do businesspeople take their clients out for a good lunch? To make them more pliable, more amenable to suggestion. Daniel could see through this strategy. He was being offered such good food as a ploy to make him more manageable in the emperor's hand. This he was not prepared to be. There may be nothing morally wrong with enjoying Babylonian luxury as such, but it represented a threat to his personal commitment that he could not risk.

A friend of mine at university was a medical student and an outstanding Christian. A brilliant fellow, he quickly went on to become a consultant. But as the years have gone by, he has become more and more spiritually dry and ineffective. A salesman I knew was wonderfully converted and became a gifted personal evangelist, but not long ago he was divorced after living for some time with another woman. What happens to such people? It seems to me that our society is more threatening to our sanctity than it has been for many generations. Worldliness has never been such a problem for the people of God. The king's food is a real temptation, as we are enticed by the affluence and the values of our pagan environment. Many, like Demas, finish up departing, having fallen in love with the present age (2 Tim 4:10).

Daniel's scruples may seem to have been over a very small matter. But if we do not draw the line somewhere, if we do not make a stand on something, then we find ourselves legitimizing our involvement in the world to an unacceptable degree, and the resulting slide may be dreadful and disastrous. It requires considerable spiritual discernment to prevent that slide into worldliness. One recalls the savage ruthlessness of Jesus' advice, "If your right eye causes you to sin, gouge it out and throw it away. . . . And if your right hand causes you to sin, cut it off and throw it away. It is better for you to lose one part of your body than for your whole body to go into hell" (Mt 5:29-30). That seems a good New Testament commentary on Daniel's example of self-denial here.

There are some things that, though they may be perfectly innocent in themselves, like the king's food, could come to undermine our Christian commitment. They could so weaken our moral fiber, provide such an invitation to compromise in our lives and so sap our spiritual resolve, that we have to deny ourselves the experience of them. There are certain books, perhaps, that may not corrupt everybody but may corrupt us; we are better not to read them. There are certain places we are better to avoid, because though at our strongest we would not be led into sin, when we are vulnerable they represent a moral hazard to us. Perhaps we need to impose limitations on our diet or on the amount of television we watch, because although there is nothing sinful in good food or the programs we prefer, such things can defile us subtly if we are not vigilant. Perhaps Christians should adopt a simpler lifestyle than our neighbors, not out of ascetic fanaticism or guilt over Third World poverty or even as a protest against the evils of capitalist consumerism, but to testify to our spiritual distinctiveness in our pagan environment, to encourage others to make their own stand in a pagan world and to guard against being sucked ourselves irresistibly downward.

Note that Daniel did not feel that as a believer he needed to opt out of Babylonian society altogether. He did not need to refuse the educational opportunity that was being given him. Perhaps he even knew that letter of the prophet Jeremiah to the exiles, which, as we saw earlier, encouraged them to settle down and seek the peace and prosperity of the city to which they had been sent. That is the right policy for Christians in exile. It was a vital piece of advice amply illustrated by Daniel's general willingness to get involved in that society, even eventually rising to high office in it. This is why as Christians we can accept employment in a secular society or pursue education in a secular university without feeling that we are necessarily compromising our Christian faith.

But if we are going to survive as believers in this increasingly pagan and pluralist world, we nevertheless have to find ways of retaining our distinctiveness as loyal subjects of our sovereign God, and that means watching out for the king's food. It can blunt our spiritual zeal. It can take the edge off our discipleship. The older Daniel would never have stood firm in the lions' den if he had not learned as a young man to say no to a much more innocuous plate of meat. If we do not learn to stick to our convictions over small issues, we shall not find the courage to do so when confronting big ones.

What Would We Die For?

Daniel, of course, was putting his life in danger by his behavior. These early chapters of the book that bears his name repeatedly invite the question: Is there anything you would be prepared to die for? I suspect that one of the deepest evidences of the decadence that affects Western culture at the end of the twentieth century is that for the vast majority of us, the answer to that question is no. There is nothing we would be prepared to die for.

A number of things have conspired to bring us to this mentality. Partly it is a widespread disillusionment with idealism. The Vietnam War and the Watergate scandal left a whole generation of young Americans cynical about politics and politicians, and radically questioning whether dying for one's country really was so noble after all. Something similar happened after the world wars in Europe, I think. Partly it was the fear of the atom bomb, and the horrific aftermath of Hiroshima, which led many in the postwar era to take the view that no tyranny is so morally objectionable as to justify nuclear holocaust. Now, partly it is due to the obsession of turn-of-the-century men and women with trying to run away from their own mortality. Fashion and advertisements for cosmetics encourage us to look young forever; advocates of diets and exercise encourage us to stay fit forever; retirement planners and financial services corporations encourage us to enjoy life forever. It is all a strategy to hide the inevitability of terminal decay in our bodies. Someone has said, "Death is the great human repression, the universal neurosis of twentieth-century man, the reality we dare not face, to escape which we summon all our resources." Such a society is unlikely to be a good breeding ground for martyrs.

But the main reason there are so few who are willing to die for a cause in our day is simply that people do not have any cause to die for. It comes back to the issue of tolerance and pluralism. People no longer believe in anything with sufficient tenacity and confidence to warrant the ultimate self-sacrifice. When all views are held to be equally valid, you can never tell others they are wrong and you can never be sure you are right. In such an atmosphere of pluralist confusion, commitment is essentially seditious and martyrdom indistinguishable from fanaticism. Anatole France expressed the mood perfectly: "To die for an idea is to set rather a high price upon a conjecture." But conjecture is all that modern men and women feel they have.

Maybe that is why those scenes in Tiananmen Square were so moving. The many young protesters against an oppressive regime seem far removed from the quiescence of young people in the West. There is something they were prepared to die for. Yet even their stirring example is not powerful enough to deliver us from our own cultural anemia. I think it probable that many in our day, even while watching the television pictures of such scenes, find a skeptical voice whispering in their ears, *But is it really worth it?* All that bloodshed, all that pain—are those lives so bravely given really going to achieve anything? Is it really better to die on your feet than live on your knees? Aren't we in the West just as politically alienated, just as materialistically discontented, just as spiritually impoverished as anyone under an oppressive regime, for all our hard-won freedoms?

We may admire the dissidents' heroism, but it is a quality to which we no longer enthusiastically aspire. That is why it has been rightly observed that the death of Western democracy is not likely to be assassination by anguish. It will be a slow extinction from apathy, indifference and undernourishment. No human being dies a martyr's death unless there is at the very core of his or her heart a passionate commitment that demands unconditional loyalty. In the absence of such commitment, moral heroism of any kind becomes impossible. No matter how fine our intellect or how highly developed our artistic sensitivities, if we lack that commitment, we lack virtue in the old sense of that word; we lack strength, dignity and guts.

The tragedy of modern Westerners is that we have run out of things we are prepared to die for. That is disastrous, because those who have nothing to die for have nothing to live for. We are either potential martyrs or potential suicides; I see no middle ground between these two. And the Bible insists that every believer in the true God has to be a potential martyr. We are the race of Abel whom his brother killed. We follow a crucified master who says, "Take up your cross."

The book of Daniel is important because it provides us with models of just such potential martyrs. The stories of Shadrach, Meshach and Abednego in their fiery furnace, and Daniel in his den of lions, undoubtedly gained importance and came to be included in the canon because of the need to give nerve to God's people in days when if they did not stand their ground as distinctive for God, they would be wiped out by cultural imperialism. Daniel and his friends were people of passionate commitment.

I suspect that the association of these stories with childhood and with Sunday school may be one of the most tragic ways we have subverted the book of Daniel. This is a book for adults, not for children at all. To turn it into a children's story is to blunt the seriousness of its message. These are stories about ruthless political tyranny, civil disobedience, religious persecution and martyrdom. They have something to say to us that we are scarcely ready for: that we must be prepared to die for Christ.

I do not find that call to martyrdom in much contemporary spirituality. The whole drift of our contemporary piety is in the opposite direction. Interestingly, some converts from New Age are complaining that they find it hard to settle in a church, either because the churches fail to offer them much to satisfy the spiritual hunger that took them into New Age in the first place or because the churches themselves have adopted New Age goals and perspectives. Discipleship has been transformed into pursuit of self-fulfillment, a search for liberation from pain, a quest for prosperity and comfort. Where in our spirituality today are the hard things that the Bible says about suffering for Christ? Far from taking seriously our call as a suffering church, our minds are full of triumphalist dreams of a victorious church that can take the country by storm.

We would do better to prepare ourselves for martyrdom. For the one thing a tolerant age cannot tolerate is a passionate commitment to absolute, ultimate truth.

Six

Obeying God Rather Than Man

DANIEL 6

*D*o you remember Mr. Bumble, in Dickens's *Oliver Twist*? It was his opinion that "the law is a ass." Sometimes I wish that the law were *only* an ass. Unfortunately, history provides us with abundant evidence of the fact that the law can on occasions become a ferocious, fire-breathing dragon that would eat harmless asses for breakfast. Thousands of innocent men and women over the centuries have been dispossessed of their property, incarcerated or executed, sometimes by barbaric cruelty, and all in the name of law and order.

Why does that sort of thing happen to a society? It happens because governments in their careless folly enact bad laws and because courts in their blinkered pedantry enforce them. But there is a deeper reason. Underlying Daniel's story of moral heroism is the implication that this sort of thing happens because human beings in their proud autonomy think they have the right to make laws in the first place. The fact is that true law is never *made* but is *found*. Its cogency rests not on the arbitrary dictates of a human legislator but on the eternal and unchanging character of God.

Down through the centuries it is possible to trace two quite distinct strands of political thought, which diverge over precisely this fundamental issue of jurisprudence. On the one hand there are advocates of what is called *positive law*. For them, law is a branch of science, a system of statutes resting on the absolute legislative authority of the state. It should be invulnerable to prejudice or circumstance, as predictable as the law of gravity and just as inexorable.

On the other hand are the advocates of *natural law*, for whom law is a branch of ethics. They emphasize the principle of equity rather than the strict letter of the law. In English law, it used to be the function of the courts of chancery under the Lord Chancellor to see that equity or fairness always prevailed, even at the risk of a certain logical inconsistency and unpredictability. But recent changes in the structure of the English judiciary have effectively done away with that role, leaving just one system of law, the statutory law of Parliament. As a result, there is now little room to redress grievances arising from intrinsic inequities in the law itself. Under the pressure of pluralism, law is having to step into the gap left by the disappearance of moral consensus. In the absence of any unifying concept of what the moral law requires, statutory legislation is having to define what we may and may not do. When we evaluate a course of action, we increasingly ask not "Is it immoral?" but "Is it illegal?"

In this situation, the story of Daniel becomes enormously relevant. It tells how an innocent man was condemned to death by a blatantly discriminatory statute that could not be abrogated. In the empire of the Medes and the Persians, the immutability of law prevailed over the intuitions of natural justice. Law was made, not found. In that respect the emperor was godlike. The arbitrary dictates of government, not the righteous character of God, were the foundation on which all law rested. (This is increasingly the case today.) Ultimately, this was the issue facing Daniel. He was not simply protesting about his right to pray to his own God. He was protesting against a view of the state that is summed up in the repeated phrase "the law of the Medes and Persians, which cannot be repealed."

The Law the Government Passed

King Darius had complete power in Babylon and could organize this province of the Medo-Persian empire as he wished. He was quick to spot the asset he had in Daniel. By this time Daniel must have been approaching eighty years of age, but he had clearly lost none of his administrative skills. In fact, he "so distinguished himself among the administrators and the satraps by his exceptional qualities that the king planned to set him over the whole kingdom" (6:3). For the original Jewish readers of this book, Daniel's record of success in the service of the Persian empire was highly relevant. As exiles, they had to decide to what extent it was right for them to get involved in pagan society. Would it compromise their faith to cooperate with the Persian imperial authority or, indeed, with the later authorities of Greece and Rome? The answer the book of Daniel provides is no. No compromise would be involved, provided they were careful to retain the moral standards God required of them.

This is a lesson of great importance for us as Christians too. One still encounters people who seem to think that the only way to serve God in a really acceptable fashion is by being a pastor or a missionary. Anything less than "full-time service" is spiritual second best. That is nonsense. Daniel, one of the greatest heroes of the Bible, held office in pagan Babylon, and that was God's calling to him, prophet though he was. The day may come when it will no longer be possible for our pastors and Christian leaders to work full time in their ministry. But that would not mean they could not exercise their ministry at all. Whatever our work may be, we are still God's servants and may well exercise an important ministry in the sphere to which he has called us. Indeed, living up to the moral standards of the Bible in the secular world, as Daniel did, provides opportunity for Christian witness that no full-time pastor or missionary can ever have.

But if we are called to serve God in such a secular environment, surrounded by the paganism of today, we must be ready to encounter hostility. Indeed, we are already beginning to experience a degree of hostility when as Christians we want to become involved in a society that no longer supports the exclusive claims of Christianity. That is what Daniel discovered.

> The administrators and the satraps tried to find grounds for charges against Daniel in his conduct of government affairs, but they were unable to do so. They could find no corruption in him, because he was trustworthy and neither corrupt nor negligent. Finally these men said, "We will never find any basis for charges against this man Daniel unless it has something to do with the law of his God." (6:4-5)

That phrase "the law of his God" is significant, because this is a story all about law: the law of Daniel's God versus the law of the Medes and Persians. These verses show us that there is nothing new about a dirty-tricks campaign. Daniel's colleagues were determined to find some way to discredit him in Darius's eyes. No doubt their animosity was motivated partly by professional jealousy. Daniel was better at his job than they were and was clearly in line to be promoted over their heads. Nobody likes that. There also may have been an element of racial prejudice. Though Daniel's Semitic origins would not have mattered to Darius, because he was a foreigner himself in Babylon, the privileged position these Jews occupied in the royal court must have been a permanent affront to the indigenous officials.

Some suggest that the action of these satraps may have been an attempt to preempt a crackdown on corruption in the civil service. They may well have anticipated that a man of Daniel's principles, once given authority over the whole province, would instigate a purge against abuses of power. Installed as governor, he would be formidable. In recent years the term *whistle-blower* has been used in connection with the exposure of abuses in the public services of Britain. There is even an organization, Whistle-Blowers Anonymous, for people who feel they have been discriminated against as a result of their determination to expose corruption and abuse at all levels of management. Perhaps these satraps perceived Daniel as a potential whistle-blower on a grand scale.

In addition to all these possible motives for their political chicanery, we must not underestimate the irrational, perhaps even demonic, element in this conspiracy. For Daniel was not just a good man; he was God's man. He was a tiresome obstacle to any satanic attempt to turn the Medo-Persian empire against the Jews and thus to thwart God's declared purpose of bringing his people back from exile. There are strong reasons, as we shall see later, for believing that Daniel's presence in Babylon and his persistence in intercessory prayer were a key element in God's strategy in that respect. Behind the envy, vindictiveness and Machiavellianism of his colleagues in office, it may very well be that Daniel was experiencing the subtle maneuverings of what the apostle Paul calls the rulers, authorities, powers of this dark world and spiritual forces of evil in the heavenly realms (Eph 6:12).

The first sordid tactic of this group of officials was that beloved of tabloid journalism: spying on Daniel's every move to see if they could rake up some muck against him. But Daniel had no skeletons hiding in his closet, so they would have to devise a way to trap him. They would engineer a situation in which, paradoxically, the very earnestness of his high principles would be the death of him: "The king should issue an edict and enforce the decree that anyone who prays to any god or human being during the next thirty days, except to you, O king, shall be thrown into the lions' den" (6:7).

Darius, manipulated by this sycophancy, did not detect the plot to which he was now unwittingly becoming an accomplice.

The policy sounded plausible, even politically prudent. It would be good for the unity of the empire, ensuring everybody's allegiance to his new regime. True, it did involve a minor infringement of personal liberty, but no reasonable person could object. After all, it was only a short-term measure. It did not require anyone actually to do anything—just to *stop* doing something for a mere thirty days. In a pluralist environment it was almost impossible to imagine that anyone could object to so innocuous a decree. A small gesture to make clear to everybody the absolute nature of Persian imperial rule—that's all it was.

By comparison with many of the insane and oppressive edicts prescribed by other ancient kings in celebration of their divinity, this was a most modest measure. Darius was in fact an enlightened king. But that is the point. Even modest and innocuous measures can become instruments of tyranny when they are enforced inflexibly and without regard to individual conscience: "The laws of the Medes and Persians . . . cannot be repealed" (6:8).

Many commentators suggest that the narrator keeps chorusing this catch phrase in order to mock the irrevocability of Medo-Persian law. Undoubtedly there is truth in that. The moral of this story is that Persian law is not as immutable as it makes out to be. But it is a mistake to caricature this aspect of Medo-Persian legislation as pompous eccentricity. I have no doubt that Cyrus had good reason for establishing such a framework of immutable statutory law in his empire. It was the largest empire the world had ever known. It welded together a host of older nations and empires, each with its own independent traditions. In such a pluralist atmosphere, it was vital to create respect for law and order.

One way of doing that was to make sure that the entire empire realized that there was only one law for everybody, with no exceptions to the rule. I am sure that this principle—that any law written down and signed by the emperor was to be enforced without fear or favor—was regarded as fine testimony to the superiority of the Persian legal system. There was a scientific rigor in it that the proponents of positive law would have found most satisfying. There could be no uncertainty regarding the law of the Medes and Persians, for it was written down. It could never be evaded by a whim of the judge, or even by the emperor himself. Law was what the government decreed.

People were entitled to their own moral opinions if they wished. Pluralist tolerance was the name of the game in the Persian empire, provided they realized that their speculations about natural justice had nothing whatsoever to do with what was legal. The unambiguous statutes of government were primary, and the imprecise arguments of moral conscience were definitely secondary. Like the law of gravity, the law of the Medes and Persians was absolutely predictable, absolutely certain. Unfortunately, for a servant of God like Daniel, such a view of law was absolutely unacceptable. He knew of a higher law, the law of God, and it was loyalty to that law of God that made him vulnerable in this pagan society. It was this that his enemies were quick to exploit.

The Law Daniel Broke

Now when Daniel learned that the decree had been published, he went home to his upstairs room where the windows opened toward Jerusalem. Three times a day he got down on his knees and prayed, giving thanks to his God, just as he had done before. (6:10)

The model of private devotion to God that Daniel provides for us here, though incidental in the plot, would have been enormously relevant to the Jews in exile. How could they retain their holiness as God's special people when all the outward trappings of religious privilege had been taken away and they were surrounded by pagan idolatry? There was no temple, no priesthood, no liturgy. The corporate worship that had been the heart of Judaism for centuries was impossible. Was it not inevitable that they would be absorbed into Babylonian culture? How could the Jews survive spiritually on their own?

Daniel quietly points to the answer: through one's private devotional life. No matter how isolated, through prayer every individual believer has personal access to God. Prayer is a vitally important component in our relationship with God because it is the one thing that can never be taken from us. Persecuting regimes can close down our churches, imprison our leaders and forbid our meetings. But they can never stop us from praying.

Notice first the regularity of Daniel's praying. This is no desperate last resort but a daily discipline. Old Testament Judaism, unlike Islam, does not prescribe the frequency of daily prayer. But clearly Daniel had decided that three times a day was a good pattern for him. I suspect we need to work out a similar plan for ourselves. How best can we schedule personal prayer into our regular routines? Daniel had devised his own personal discipline of prayer to help him survive in the pagan society to which he belonged.

Notice second the posture of Daniel's praying: he got down on his knees. Again, there is no rule in Scripture that says we should sit or stand or kneel when praying, but I do not think this means that posture is of no significance. The point here is this: Daniel was an important official. Juniors got down on their knees to him, or even fell prostrate before him. That was the standard way to approach a person of senior rank in the Babylonian and Persian empires. Clearly, Daniel felt it important when he approached God consciously to abandon any trace of pride that his secular vocation may have engendered in him, and to adopt the body language of supplication and humiliation before God that others had to adopt before him. He knew he was addressing the real King when he prayed. So he got down on his knees.

It is probably true that the richer, cleverer and more powerful we are in worldly terms, the more important it is for us to get down on our knees when we pray—and the less congenial it may feel!

Third, notice the direction of Daniel's praying. The windows of his prayer room opened toward Jerusalem. That was important, especially when we learn what kind of prayer he was offering at this vital time in his life: a prayer of confession for the sins of his people (see Daniel 9). He was recognizing before God that they were being punished in exile for their moral and spiritual apostasy, according to the covenant law of Moses. It was a prayer too of petition, pleading the promise of God through Jeremiah that the exile would be of limited duration. "The first year of Darius" (9:1) marked a change in the political climate of Babylon, and Daniel prayed that in the providential mercy of God there would be a speedy restoration of the Jews to their homeland. Daniel was a political strategist and understood the times in which he lived. He saw that this change of regime could well be the means God would use to bring the Jews home. The new regime was more liberal than Nebuchadnezzar's. This could be the signal that the prophecy of Jeremiah would come true, and Daniel was praying most earnestly that in the mercy of God it might be so.

Daniel's prayer was no self-indulgent meditation. He was not concerned with himself and his feelings. His prayer shows him engaging as a prophet in a crucial intercessory role on behalf of God's people, beseeching him to fulfill his plan for them. No satanically inspired conspiracy was going to stop him praying for this.

That is the fourth feature we should notice: the resolution of Daniel's praying. When he learned that the decree had been published, he went to his upstairs room where the windows opened toward Jerusalem, and three times a day he got down on his knees and prayed.

I have no doubt that a man as sharp as Daniel knew exactly what his rivals were up to. He had been in politics all his life; he knew a setup when he saw it. But he deliberately refused to be intimidated. It would have been so easy to stop praying for the thirty-day period. After all, he had chosen to pray in this way, and he could choose not to do so. It would not be a sin. There was no verse in the Bible that said, "Thou shalt have a quiet time three times a day."

At the very least he could have changed the venue. He could have gone somewhere a little less obvious or prayed in a different place every day for security reasons. But that would have been a sellout. For Daniel prayer was the bottom line in this situation. Any government that tried to make prayer illegal had to be disobeyed, for it was clear that such a government had a completely erroneous and unacceptable view of its legislative power. Darius had to discover that there was a higher law than the law of the emperor.

Daniel's civil disobedience was not particularly loud. The observation that the windows opened toward Jerusalem probably implied that Daniel could be seen from the street by those who were nosy enough to look, but I think it would be quite wrong to conclude, as some have done, that there was anything ostentatious about Daniel's prayer times. On the contrary, it seems to me, his policy was to go on praying inconspicuously in his own home, as he had done before. There was nothing deliberately provocative or defiant. He just went on doing what he had always done.

In so doing Daniel exposes the cowardice of so much of our Christian testimony. Many of us avoid nailing our colors to the mast. We do not want people to see us praying under any circumstances. It is far too embarrassing. John Stott compares us to frightened rabbits who spend their days furiously looking for Christian burrows to hide in for spiritual safety. Our lives are carefully structured so as to render us invisible to the surrounding world. Not so Daniel; he knew his rivals had been trying to frame him, but he did not attempt to stop them or to foil their little plot. He went on putting God first through his regular times of prayer and waited for events to unfold. King Darius, unaware of the situation, had fallen into the trap of positive law. He had failed to realize that there is a sovereign God in heaven who overrules the actions of human beings and whose law takes precedence over every human government—a God who cannot be thwarted, even by the law of the Medes and Persians. It was

Daniel's business to testify to that sovereign God and his law in the public arena where God had placed him.

The Law God Overruled

Then these men went as a group and found Daniel praying and asking God for help. So they went to the king and spoke to him about his royal decree: "Did you not publish a decree that during the next thirty days anyone who prays to any god or man except to you, O king, would be thrown into the lions' den?"

The king answered, "The decree stands—in accordance with the laws of the Medes and Persians, which cannot be repealed."

Then they said to the king, "Daniel, who is one of the exiles from Judah, pays no attention to you, O king, or to the decree you put in writing. He still prays three times a day." When the king heard this, he was greatly distressed; he was determined to rescue Daniel and made every effort until sundown to save him. (6:11-14)

Now it becomes clear that it is not just Daniel who has been trapped. The king has suddenly discovered he is the victim of the inflexibility of his own judicial system. Desperately he consults with his legal advisers to find some loophole in this situation. But no. The empire is committed to the ideological doctrine of positive law, and no matter how unfair the king thinks it is, no matter how contrary to natural justice, the rule of law must stand. If he spares Daniel, the whole credibility of Persian law and order will be thrown in doubt. He cannot afford to lose face like that. People must know that if they disobey his command they will pay the price. To go soft is to invite wholesale anarchy. Tell people they are free to do as their conscience directs, to offend the law on the grounds of their religion or their morality, and the whole empire will fragment.

If the civil service had been behind Darius in this matter, I suppose they might have succeeded in hushing up the whole affair. But it was obvious to Darius that Daniel's rivals had engineered this situation and they were not going to let the emperor off the hook: "The men went as a group to the king and said to him, 'Remember, O king, that according to the law of the Medes and Persians no decree or edict that the king issues can be changed'" (6:15). There was no way that he was going to be able to coverup this particular issue. After an entire day of frantic legal consultation, Darius realizes he is in a political corner with no way out.

> So the king gave the order, and they brought Daniel and threw him into the lions' den. The king said to Daniel, "May your God, whom you serve continually, rescue you!"
>
> A stone was brought and placed over the mouth of the den, and the king sealed it with his own signet ring and with the rings of his nobles, so that Daniel's situation might not be changed. Then the king returned to his palace and spent the night without eating and without any entertainment being brought to him. And he could not sleep. (6:16-18)

The hunting of lions was a royal sport in the Persian empire, so it was not strange that Darius had a private supply of these beasts. It says much for the humanity of the man that he suffered such pangs of guilt and anxiety that night that he was unable to eat, sleep or be distracted by entertainment. He was surely cursing under his breath for playing into the hands of his civil service in this way and for trying to play God. It was infantile and he should have recognized it for the ploy it was. But now it was too late. Unless . . . unless Daniel's God really was as mighty as he said. The king went to see.

> At the first light of dawn, the king got up and hurried to the lions' den. When he came near the den, he called to Daniel in an anguished voice, "Daniel, servant of the living God, has your God, whom you serve continually, been able to rescue you from the lions?"
>
> Daniel answered, "O king, live forever! My God sent his angel, and he shut the mouths of the lions. They have not hurt me. . . ." The king was overjoyed. (6:19-23)

It is not hard to imagine what a boost this climax to the adventure would have been to the morale of those exiled Jews. The Bible never promises that when the people of God stand up for him faithfully, risking their lives, the outcome will always be a happy one. It is no accident that the Greek word for "witness" gives us our word *martyr.*

There are Christians who forget this and claim deliverance in all kinds of circumstances, insisting that we should believe unconditionally that God is going to deliver us from our problems. When such prayers fail, they blame it on lack of faith. If we had believed God enough, they say, we would have received what we prayed for. That is not biblical religion but superstition that treats prayer like a magic spell and puts the divine power at human disposal.

But we human beings are not wise enough to have unconditional access to omnipotence. If God were to answer our prayers of faith unconditionally, the results would be appalling. Thank God our prayers will be answered only in accordance with his will, and there is no lack of faith in confessing that fact. The Master himself qualifies his prayer in the Garden of Gethsemane: "Father, if you are willing, take this cup from me; yet not my will, but yours be done" (Lk 22:42). The object of biblical faith is God in his sovereign power and his sovereign purpose. True faith is always submissive to that divine purpose. The eleventh chapter of Hebrews catalogs plenty of God's servants who were not rescued as Daniel was rescued but who are nevertheless commended for their faith.

Having said that, though, it is clear that Daniel's miraculous deliverance is intended for our encouragement. The law of the Medes and Persians was not as unchangeable as they made out. The sovereign penal sanctions of God turned hungry lions into docile pets. God turns the immutable statute of Darius against those who had proposed its enactment: "At the king's command, the men who had falsely accused Daniel were brought in and thrown into the lions' den, along with their wives and children"

(6:24). Cruel, undoubtedly, but in the ancient world such poetic justice was considered a necessary deterrent against malicious accusation and false testimony.

The final irony is that Darius issues another, presumably immutable, written edict, not this time forbidding prayer to Daniel's God but commanding it. If you cannot repeal an act, pass another that contradicts it, and then let the jurists of positive law sort it out!

King Darius wrote to all the peoples, nations and men of every language throughout the land:

"May you prosper greatly!

"I issue a decree that in every part of my kingdom people must fear and reverence the God of Daniel.

"For he is the living God
    and he endures forever;
his kingdom will not be destroyed,
    his dominion will never end.
He rescues and he saves;
    he performs signs and wonders
    in the heavens and on the earth.
He has rescued Daniel
    from the power of the lions." (6:25-27)

Who Makes the Rules?

This story of Daniel has many valuable lessons for us: the validity of a Christian's secular calling in a pagan society; the importance of our private devotional life, particularly when we have to survive without the support of corporate worship in a pagan society; and the reassuring truths that God is sovereign over all human affairs and that no ultimate harm can come to a believer, even if we are called to be faithful to the point of death, as Daniel was. But the lesson I want to draw out supremely is the importance of Daniel's stand against the godless arrogance of positive law: the idea that law is devised by the ruling authorities and must be imposed rigidly.

God's law and godless law. The ultimate cause of many miscarriages of justice is not that governments enact bad laws or that courts enforce them, but that governments in their proud autonomy think they have the right to make law in the first place. They have no such right. The cogency of true law rests not on the arbitrary dictates of a human legislature but on the eternal and unchanging character of God.

In earlier centuries, jurists understood this. Sir William Blackstone was one of the early architects of the British Constitution. In his great work *Commentaries on the Laws of England,* he argues that the Ten Commandments are the foundation on which English common law rests and that no government legislation may contradict those commandments. The same goes for the United States. It is a fundamental principle of the American Constitution that there is a law higher than itself from which "inalienable" human rights derive. Throughout British and American history the issue of liberty has turned on this conviction that there is a law higher than that of the state. One may call it natural justice, equity or conscience. The Bible calls it the law of God. It derives from God's eternal character. There can be no free society unless the superiority of that claim is acknowledged.

When that claim is not acknowledged, the results are dire. German lawyers in the 1930s were among the most extreme advocates of what is now called positive law. Many of them learned to their dismay how such an emphasis can lead a people to moral blindness, for the Nazis deliberately exploited the German attitude of subservience to statutory law. And as in Daniel's case, it was the Jews who were the chief target of their malicious abuse of the legal system. The Bill of Rights, a fundamental legal instrument in the European Court of Human Rights in Strasbourg, was born out of that experience. The statutes of Hitler were contrary to justice and should not have been obeyed, declared the judges at the Nuremberg trials. But they had to appeal to natural law to arrive at such a verdict.

It would be naive to think that a Bill of Rights can infallibly preserve us from such abuses in the future. The expansion of positive law continues. In Britain, legislation in Parliament is what gives rise to it. Increasingly the House of Commons is the only body that can prescribe the law of the land. In the United States, the Supreme Court, in its binding interpretations of the Constitution, fulfills a rather similar function. On both sides of the Atlantic, the attitude is growing that human authority has the power to make law as it pleases in accordance with the government's ideological goals or the nation's sociological trends. No Bill of Rights or Constitution, no independent judiciary even, is a guarantee against that.

Positive law is fundamentally godless, and freedom can be sustained only as long as legislature and judiciary, and the people themselves, feel themselves accountable to a higher law, the law of God. I suspect that democracy itself is impossible without such a theistic system underlying a national moral consensus. In the absence of that self-regulating moral consensus within society, positive law inevitably steps in as a cramping, burdensome leviathan, and an overregulated society emerges, open to tyranny or anarchy or both.

God's law and the state. Christians, of all people, should know how dangerous it is to obey the state too well. Christians, of all people, should know how easily the state, which God appoints to execute his wrath on the wrongdoer, is transformed into the beast that cruelly persecutes the people of God. Christians, of all people, should know how subtly Satan insinuates himself on the side of law and order. For we honor a Lord who, just like Daniel, was the victim of an establishment plot. Because he set his face to go to Jerusalem, he found himself hounded to the scaffold in the name of justice: "We have a law, and according to that law he must die" (Jn 19:7).

They had a law, but it was not the law of God. Pilate should have known this. Deep in his heart he did know it, but like Darius he was too weak or too enmeshed in the constructs of his own legal system to overrule the injustice. "You would have no power over me if it were not given to you from above," Jesus told him (Jn 19:11). He was trying to help Pilate see the claim of the higher law over him. But such arguments regarding the higher law were lost on that pragmatic governor. So Jesus died, one more victim of judicial murder, the most innocent man who has ever lived. Like Daniel he organized no revolution, he staged no public protest, he barely even spoke in his own defense. Like Daniel he just prayed, "Your will be done."

They put a stone over his tomb and sealed it, just as they sealed the lions' den. They made sure it was all legal and aboveboard and nobody could tamper with the evidence. But the higher law could not be set aside in that contemptuous fashion. Christ had come to proclaim the kingdom of God, and the sovereign rule of God was demonstrated in his mighty resurrection. He broke the chains of death to affirm the unchallengeable superiority of God's sovereign claim over our lives: "All authority in heaven and on earth has been given to me" (Mt 28:18).

From that empty cross a stream of faithful men and women has issued down through the ages who have been courageous witnesses to his supreme authority. Jesus is the only Lord. We Christians are not rebels, but we must obey God rather than human beings. Like Daniel we want to see our society ruled with integrity and faithfulness, and we shall cooperate in that with our very best endeavors. But we will not bow to the tyranny of godless law.

Every day we confess our prior and unconditional loyalty to the kingdom of the living God, the God who endures forever, as Darius calls him. Consequently, there are certain kinds of political regime and social climate where if a servant of God is to maintain his or her integrity, prison or the scaffold is inevitable. That is the absolutist and exclusive nature of our faith. We insist that there is a truth we must be willing to die for.

I do not pen these words lightly, but any weakness in our resolve on this point will leave us vulnerable in the hour of trial, in these last days when paganism rules. It is all too easy to sacrifice integrity and consistency for the sake of expediency and survival. Three centuries ago, the fabled vicar of Bray in Berkshire held on to his position from the reign of Charles II to George I. During his period in office he changed his creed from Catholic to Protestant and back to Catholic again with every wind of change in the monarchy. When charged with fickleness, his reply was "Not so, for I always kept my principle, which is this—to live and die the Vicar of Bray."

No such tactics are observable in this story of Daniel. People of his stamp are those who, like Peter, must declare, "Judge for yourselves whether it is right in God's sight to obey you rather than God" (Acts 4:19).

Notice that when a Christian dissents in this way it is not in the name of some alternative ideology. We do not disobey the government, if forced into that situation, simply because it is not sufficiently democratic for our taste. Godly governments are not godly by virtue of the way they are appointed but by virtue of the way they perceive their own authority. A godly government is one that perceives itself as accountable to the higher law. It is when the state no longer regards itself in that light that Christian protest is vital. Christian defiance of the state is never in the name of the sovereignty of the people, that cruelest of all tyrannies. It is in the name of the sovereignty of God that the Christian must sometimes say no.

Down through the centuries many such brave Christians have eschewed the easy path of compromise and safety and, like Daniel, have defied the king's command. Refusing to overrule their consciences, they have drawn a line and declared, "Here is an issue we must make a stand for, even at the cost of our lives."

The question that haunts me at the beginning of the twenty-first century is whether, with the advance of secularism, pluralism

and the increasing paganization of our society, we are returning
to a day when such a stand will be necessary. If so, we are painfully
short of men and women ready to make it. Edmund Burke, in
the eighteenth century, said that the only thing necessary for the
triumph of evil is that good men do nothing, while in our own
time John F. Kennedy commented that the hottest places in hell
are reserved for those who in time of great moral crisis maintain
their neutrality. One recalls the German churches' "Declaration
of Guilt" framed by Lutheran pastor Martin Niemöller. It runs
like this:

> When Hitler attacked the Jews I was not a Jew, therefore, I was
> not concerned. And when Hitler attacked the Catholics, I was
> not a Catholic, and therefore, I was not concerned. And when
> Hitler attacked the unions and the industrialists, I was not a
> member of the unions and I was not concerned. Then Hitler
> attacked me and the Protestant church—and there was no-
> body left to be concerned.

The British Constitution, no matter how much we respect and
admire it, can no more deliver us from tyranny than the law of
the Medes and Persians could deliver Daniel. The freedom of
this land has been purchased by the brave defiance of those who
refused to conform to the requirements of an erring establishment—people with the courage of a Daniel. In the twenty-
first century we may need to pay the price again. "Be faithful,
even to the point of death," Jesus urged believers in the first
century, "and I will give you the crown of life" (Rev 2:10). We
Christians are different because we have a cause worth dying for.

Christ does not ask of us the foolhardy bravado of the dare-
devil who risks his life for nothing, but he does ask of us the sane,
thoughtful and sober courage of the martyr who is prepared to
give his life for everything. That is what the gospel has always
demanded as the price of discipleship.

Seven

Sovereign over the Kingdoms on Earth

DANIEL 4

*I*n this chapter and the next we look at the stories of two proud men, one mercifully saved from his arrogance, the other destroyed by it. The narrator deliberately puts their experiences side by side so that we may compare their responses and their fates. The lesson of these stories of Nebuchadnezzar and Belshazzar is that we serve a God who will not tolerate human arrogance. He exalts the humble and scatters the proud.

The Man Who Had It All

"I could never imagine him (or her) becoming a Christian!" Most of us probably know people we would describe in that way. I shared lodgings with one such, Robert, as a student. He knew I was religious, but I sensed no hostility from him because of that. If anything, he pitied me as one of those pathetic wimps who cannot get through life without the crutch of faith. He preferred to stand on his own feet, and he did, very successfully. Robert seemed to have the Midas touch; everything turned to gold for him. He excelled at sports, in exams and with women. When I last heard of him some years ago, it was no surprise to learn that he was excelling in his career too, and earning a mint as a result.

I used to pray for Robert sometimes, but if I am honest, I have to say that my prayers always lacked conviction. He was so supremely confident, independent and secure—a real high-flier who needed nothing and nobody to make his life complete. As I watched him and talked with him, I could detect no chink in his armor of self-sufficiency. He was right: what use would God be to him? No way could I imagine him ever becoming a Christian.

The story of Nebuchadnezzar has some relevance to such a situation. This great man, this confident man, who needed nothing and nobody to make his life complete, was nevertheless humbled and brought to confess a personal faith in God.

The story is divided into three acts. Act 1, by far the longest, recollects the remarkable rebuke this proud man received (4:4-27). The story concludes with Act 3, a confession of the vital lesson in humility that rebuke eventually taught him (4:34-37). Between these two acts we are presented with an extraordinary account of a monumental disaster, which Nebuchadnezzar had to suffer before his foolish pride was broken (4:28-33). Because he ignored God's warning, he could not learn the lesson without this bitter experience.

For the Jews, living in exile under the domination of a vast pagan empire, this was a hugely encouraging story. It showed them that nobody, no matter how lofty their status, no matter how impregnable their self-esteem, was beyond the reach of God's arm. For us too, surrounded by the pluralism of the late twentieth century, it brings a similar reassurance. Even the Roberts of this world can be converted. But to bring this about, God may sometimes have to use quite rough tactics.

Act 1: The Rebuke Nebuchadnezzar Received

> I, Nebuchadnezzar, was at home in my palace, contented and
> prosperous. I had a dream that made me afraid. As I was lying
> in my bed, the images and visions that passed through my
> mind terrified me. (4:4-5)

This was not the first time that Nebuchadnezzar had suffered
insomnia due to nightmares. Back in chapter 2 he was troubled
by a dream that was not unlike the one he goes on to relate here.
That time he had seen a great colossus fashioned in strata of gold,
silver, bronze, iron and clay, which was supernaturally demol-
ished by a flying rock. This time it is a tree that he sees. Even
larger than the statue, it dominated the entire globe. But it too
is felled by divine command and reduced to a mere stump in the
ground.

The reader needs no spiritual gift or expertise in Freudian
psychology to detect in both these dreams the repressed fears of
a powerful man who is haunted by morbid premonitions of the
collapse of his empire. The more powerful he grows, the more
paranoid he becomes about the possibility of all his achievements falling apart. According to psychiatrists, dreams of falling
are common among those given to delusions of grandeur, as
Nebuchadnezzar clearly was. Though outwardly at ease in the
comfort and security of his royal fortress, during the hours of
darkness the secret fears of his subconscious mind began to take
shape in the surrealist symbols of his nightmares and to reduce
him to a state of acute anxiety.

There was no Valium in those days, of course, but they did have
the ancient equivalent of psychotherapy, and Nebuchadnezzar was
not slow to summon the practitioners of the various Babylonian
schools of counseling to give him the benefit of their advice.

> So I commanded that all the wise men of Babylon be brought
> before me to interpret the dream for me. When the magicians,
> enchanters, astrologers and diviners came, I told them the
> dream, but they could not interpret it for me. (4:6-7)

From time immemorial people of many cultures have recognized that there is something mysterious, even mystical, about dreams. This "something" requires interpretation. These days the interpreter is likely to be a psychologist, and the meaning he or she discovers in the dream will probably relate to subconscious desires and fears. In ancient Babylon the interpretation of dreams was the province of fortunetellers. In the ancient Middle East generally, dreams were believed to provide some glimpse, albeit in symbolic form, of events yet to come.

It could be that the ancient and the modern ways of understanding dreams are not necessarily incompatible. We may have more insight into the consequences of our actions and the roots of our behavior than we are prepared to admit in waking thought. So it would not be too surprising if unpalatable intuitions, repressed below the level of our conscious minds, come back to haunt us in the images of our nightmares. Shakespeare clearly believed this: Macbeth dreamed of blood and Shylock of moneybags, and both saw these dreams as omens of doom. In that sense, we may all dream our future destinies in some measure.

In addition, there does seem to be some experimental evidence to confirm that on rare occasions, individuals do receive in their dreams an uncanny premonition about the future. In *An Experiment with Time* (1927), J. W. Dunne recounts a number of such experiences and offers a naturalistic explanation of them. Drawing on Einstein's theory of relativity, he suggests that in sleep we may be able to travel along the fourth dimension, time, and so dream things before we actually experience them in normal existence. This, he says, may be what lies behind the familiar experience of déjà vu.

Whether there is any truth in that speculation I have no idea, but it is certainly undeniable that down through the ages people have believed that dreams do reveal something about the future. In ancient Babylon, the interpretation of dreams followed a scientific system. Their technique seems to have been to compile vast catalogs of dreams together with the events that each dream, it was believed, proved to have portended. When the sages were consulted about a new dream, they searched their reference books to discover which of the dreams on record was the nearest equivalent to the one they were trying to understand. They then tried to guess the future portended by the new dream and thus sought to expand their expertise in dream reading.

There was nothing necessarily occult about this brand of Babylonian lore. It was not substantially different from the primitive meteorology found among country folk who try to anticipate the weather by observing the behavior of animals or the pain in their big toe. I suspect that is why Daniel felt he could take a course in interpretation of dreams as part of his degree in Chaldean studies without jeopardizing his spiritual integrity or involving himself in the black arts.

But it is clear that this science had its limitations. That is rather reassuring. These wise men of Babylon had to confess themselves stuck when it came to this particular dream. They could not make sense of it. In spite of all their ministrations, Nebuchadnezzar's anxiety symptoms were unabated. He was convinced that this was no ordinary dream. As with that dream of the golden-headed colossus all those years before, there was something uncanny, something ominous, about this dream. Something important was going to befall him, he was sure—something so unusual that there were no precedents in the textbooks of ancient Babylonian lore. Nebuchadnezzar realized that it would take the divine inspiration of a prophet to unravel this dream.

Fortunately there was such a man in Babylon: Daniel, the man who had helped the emperor with that first enigmatic nightmare long before. On that occasion he had been a young postgraduate student. Now he had risen to be senior professor of the entire university, but he was as quick to respond to this nocturnal emergency in the royal court as he had been before.

Finally, Daniel came into my presence and I told him the dream. (He is called Belteshazzar, after the name of my god, and the spirit of the holy gods is in him.)

I said, "Belteshazzar, chief of the magicians, I know that the spirit of the holy gods is in you, and no mystery is too difficult for you. Here is my dream; interpret it for me." (4:8-9)

The king goes on to recount the dream in detail, and Daniel, with much trepidation, offers the meaning. There are two aspects of Daniel's handling of the situation that are particularly noteworthy.

The first is his personal distress on hearing the dream. Indeed, so disturbed is he that the king feels moved to reverse the roles and play counselor to him.

Then Daniel . . . was greatly perplexed for a time, and his thoughts terrified him. So the king said, "Belteshazzar, do not let the dream or its meaning alarm you."

Belteshazzar answered, "My lord, if only the dream applied to your enemies and its meaning to your adversaries!" (4:19)

A cynic might argue that this discomfort on Daniel's part was feigned, a clever ploy to disarm the anger of the emperor, which he knew from past experience might well erupt when he heard the unfavorable nature of the interpretation. There may be an element of truth in that, but I am inclined to think that Daniel was genuinely distraught. By this time he had been in the service of this king for many years and had no doubt developed a sincere affection for his master, perhaps even a profound gratitude to God for the degree of liberty that the Jewish community enjoyed under his rule. Nebuchadnezzar may have been a despot, but he was a comparatively enlightened one. He had learned from the testimony and survival of Daniel's colleagues Shadrach, Meshach and Abednego, whom he had consigned to the blazing furnace. Moreover, Daniel was a scholar of history. He knew perfectly well that the political situation could and would be much worse in Nebuchadnezzar's absence, yet a period of absence was precisely what this dream threatened. Daniel was deeply troubled at the thought of it.

That brings me to the second aspect of his handling of the situation: his brutal candor in conveying the dream's warning.

> This is the interpretation, O king, and this is the decree the Most High has issued against my lord the king: You will be driven away from people and will live with the wild animals; you will eat grass like cattle and be drenched with the dew of heaven. Seven times will pass by for you until you acknowledge that the Most High is sovereign over the kingdoms of men and gives them to anyone he wishes. . . . Therefore, O king, be pleased to accept my advice. (4:24-25, 27)

By all the canons of ancient protocol, these words are highly impertinent and dangerous. Daniel is talking to the most powerful man in the world, an absolute dictator, well known for his irrational outbursts of rage and quite capable of ordering anyone's execution on the spot. Yet Daniel reprimands him for his tyrannical and unjust use of royal power. "Renounce your sins by doing what is right, and your wickedness by being kind to the oppressed," he urges the king (4:27). Like Nathan before King David, like Elijah before King Ahab, like Jeremiah before King Jehoiakim, Daniel here calls the great of the earth to recognize their accountability to the God by whose grace they possess their vast domain. He summons them to acknowledge that higher law of which we thought in the last chapter: "Seven times will pass by for you until you acknowledge that the Most High is sovereign over the kingdoms of men and gives them to anyone he wishes" (4:25).

Observe the balance in Daniel's conduct here. On the one hand he is personally distressed by what he has to say, but on the other he is brutally candid in saying it. In that respect Daniel provides us with an important model of what sound counseling must always be like. I suspect that the narrator intends us to gain courage and wisdom from Daniel's example in our dealings with people. Some Christians are too confrontational in the way they handle people with personal problems. They fulminate in a sanctimonious and unsympathetic way about sin and, one suspects, gain a good deal of private satisfaction from their smug posturing. It is no surprise that their pious rebukes, as often as not, merely serve to reinforce the emotional defenses of those they are trying to counsel. But equally, some other Christians are not confrontational enough. They have read so much about modern nondirective counseling that they assume the role of a purely passive listener, unwilling to offer advice, let alone admonition, no matter how much the person may need it.

Daniel shows us the balance. He listens patiently while the king talks at length. People who are distressed frequently do talk at length. Daniel communicates his own interest in and empathy with the king's feelings of anxiety both by his words and by his facial expressions. He is no clinical expert maintaining a professional distance from his client. Still less is he a self-righteous prig who enjoys the opportunity to issue moralizing judgments. No, he is emotionally involved with the situation and personally burdened by the king's predicament. He communicates all this to the king in the way he behaves.

Yet he refuses to allow his feelings to deter him from plain speaking. He is absolutely frank about placing responsibility firmly and squarely on the king's own shoulders. "This is your problem, Nebuchadnezzar," he says in effect. "Would that it were anybody else, O king! But I must speak the truth in love. God sees pride in your life; he doesn't like it, and he plans to judge it. You heard the interpretation yourself in the dream. The Most High is sovereign over the kingdoms on earth and gives them to whomever he chooses. The divine decree is that your kingdom, Nebuchadnezzar, is going to be taken away from you and will not be restored until you are prepared to bow the knee to this sovereign God and confess that it is he, not you, who ultimately rules this world. But there's nothing fatalistic about the dream's pronouncement. If you change your behavior and accept God's verdict, then it may be that your prosperity will continue. God's decree is not a sentence but a notice of intention to prosecute. You must do something about it, O king."

With bated breath we await the king's response. But our narrator is far too good a dramatist to steal the power of Daniel's great oration by anticlimax, so instead he abruptly changes the scene to introduce Act 2 of the story.

Act 2: The Disaster Nebuchadnezzar Suffered

All this happened to King Nebuchadnezzar. Twelve months later, as the king was walking on the roof of the royal palace of Babylon, he said, "Is not this the great Babylon I have built as the royal residence, by my mighty power and for the glory of my majesty?"

The words were still on his lips when a voice came from heaven, "This is what is decreed for you, King Nebuchadnez-zar . . ." (4:28-31)

Many scholars are skeptical of the historicity of these verses and the incident they refer to on two grounds. First, there is no independent corroboration of Nebuchadnezzar's illness in ancient Babylonian records, and second, it is difficult to imagine Nebuchadnezzar sustaining his remarkable political and military achievement single-handedly while vulnerable to such a serious mental illness. They suggest that the story is wishful thinking on the part of some fanciful Jewish novelist.

The answer to those two objections is not hard to find. First, it is scarcely surprising that there are no Babylonian accounts of this incident. No Babylonian documents dealing with the latter part of Nebuchadnezzar's life have so far been discovered, and even if they existed, would we really expect the historians of Babylon to include this incident in their official chronicles? The affair must have been singularly embarrassing to the entire imperial court and would certainly have been hushed up for fear of opportunists taking advantage of the temporary political vacuum that Nebuchadnezzar's illness occasioned.

Indeed, I doubt whether 4:28-33 is part of Nebuchadnezzar's own encyclical, which begins in the first person: "I, Nebuchadnezzar . . ." It also ends in the first person, from verse 34 onward. But 4:28-33, the record of the onset and progress of his illness, is in the third person. Some commentators suggest that this is because Nebuchadnezzar's personality was so depreciated during this period that it all felt as if these bizarre events had happened to somebody else, and so he describes them in a deliberately detached manner. Others suggest that he may have been relying on the evidence of others for this period of his life because he himself had no memory of it.

But I am inclined to believe that the narrator of Daniel has himself inserted this account of what really happened, for the benefit of those who previously had had only the official communiqués from the imperial press office—the ones that said the king was "temporarily indisposed." "Now that the king is publishing his own account, I can fill you in on the details," the narrator is saying in effect. "The truth is that this great king, quite unexpectedly, suffered a major mental breakdown, which for a while turned him into a wild and disheveled lunatic."

That brings me to the second ground upon which scholars are sometimes skeptical of the story: the impossibility, they say, of believing that a man of the status of Nebuchadnezzar could have had a constitution vulnerable to a mental breakdown of this magnitude.

Frankly, in my view the wishful thinking here lies not with the Jewish narrator but with the biblical critics. It is certainly possible that a man like Nebuchadnezzar could have had a fragile psyche, as experience in pastoral counseling bears out.

There are two kinds of pride. The first kind is that of the egoist. He has an extraordinarily strong sense of self, to the point that he is completely indifferent to both the praise and the criticism of others. He lives his life without reference to anybody but himself. I suspect Max Stirner's *The Ego and His Own* (1845) is the most outstanding example in literature of this kind of egomania. "I do not demand any rights," says Stirner, "therefore I need not recognize any either. What I can get by force, I get by force; what I do not get by force, I have no right to." That kind of true egoism is mentally resilient, but it is also, thankfully, rare.

A far more common form of pride is that of the narcissist. Narcissus, in Greek mythology, was a youth who fell in love with his own reflection. Psychologists observe a similar kind of self-obsession. In fact, many would argue that it is becoming a characteristic feature of the turn-of-the-century personality. Narcissism is identified by an extraordinarily *weak* sense of self, which causes people to be pathetically dependent on the approval and esteem of others. While they often do project a powerful impression of self-confidence, this is nothing but a psychological defense against their true feelings of inner helplessness and vulnerability. Such people frequently indulge in grandiose fantasies about their own omnipotence, but they are hypersensitive to criticism. Despite their insatiable appetite for praise and admiration, they may often find themselves in private staring into a mirror, not for reasons of vanity but to reassure themselves. If they begin to feel that their mirror is cracking, their popularity fading and their fans forsaking them, then their whole personality can implode into a state of acute depression and paranoia. Narcissists, unlike egoists, are incredibly fragile, and though they may frequently be stars who revel in the limelight and possess a consuming ambition to get to the top, they are inwardly all too vulnerable to mental breakdown.

Undoubtedly Nebuchadnezzar's pride was of this second type. His was not the overweening self-confidence of the true egoist. His was the tissue-thin façade hiding the insecurity of the narcissist, and he suffered the fate that that type of personality so often does suffer. There is nothing essentially unbelievable about his insanity at all. In fact, the most extraordinary thing is that he ever recovered from it.

Clearly he fell victim to a major psychotic breakdown. There is some debate about the duration of his illness; the "seven times" (4:32) could mean seven seasons or seven years, or it could just be an idiomatic expression meaning a period of indeterminate length. But however long it was, it was long enough for his physical appearance to degenerate to such an extent that he looked barely human: "He was driven away from people and ate grass like cattle. His body was drenched with the dew of heaven until his hair grew like the feathers of an eagle and his nails like the claws of a bird" (4:33).

Although the behavior described here seems bizarre, it is not totally unfamiliar to psychiatry, though modern antipsychotic drugs mean that it is rarely seen these days. Technically it is called *lycanthropy* and is a feature of some serious mental illnesses in which the subject believes that he has been turned into a wild animal and behaves as such, perhaps acting out some of his fantasies and delusions in the form of an animal. Nebuchadnezzar seems to have done that, identifying with some kind of herbivore, perhaps a bull or a stag.

It is tempting to try to classify the illness even more precisely. We are not short of evidence that the king suffered from a high degree of emotional instability: his irrational swings of mood, his paralyzing anxiety attacks, his paranoid suspicions, his megalomaniac delusions of grandeur, his propensity to vivid dreams or even hallucinations. Was he a manic depressive, or even a schizophrenic? Such people do have occasional episodes of insanity followed by spontaneous remissions, after all. But we cannot know.

All we can say for sure is that Nebuchadnezzar succumbed to a sudden and very serious mental illness, which he believed (and which Scripture confirms) was directly related to his narcissistic pride. Its onset took place as he was walking on the roof of his royal palace and saying, "Is not this the great Babylon I have built as the royal residence, by my mighty power and for the glory of my majesty?" (4:30). He was gazing at Babylon as the narcissist gazes into a mirror, to see the reflection of his own greatness and gain reassurance of his majesty.

He had been given every opportunity to avoid the divine stroke. There was that occasion years before when he first met Daniel and had his earlier dream interpreted by him. He had learned from that that there was a supreme God in heaven, the Lord of all earthly monarchs, who alone could reveal the destiny of empires. Then there was that memorable encounter with Shadrach, Meshach and Abednego, Daniel's friends, who had refused point-blank to worship his golden idol (another symbol of his megalomania) and found supernatural deliverance from the blazing furnace into which he had cast them. He learned then that this supreme God was no astral deity confined to heaven but that he intervened in the personal experience of human beings who trusted in him. Finally, there was that nightmare he had had twelve months before, which again Daniel had interpreted. He had learned then that this supreme God intended to judge him if he did not repent of his arrogance.

Though Nebuchadnezzar had been genuinely influenced by all these experiences, he had not been converted by them. His paganism had been modified but not abandoned. The God of the Jews had gained his official approval but not yet his personal surrender. Nebuchadnezzar still would not yield up his treasured delusion that he was a self-made man. He still desperately needed to believe in himself. He would not let go of his pride. The lessons and warnings of the past had been forgotten or ignored. God's patience was exhausted, and he decided that it was time to show this self-inflated mere mortal who really was sovereign over the kingdoms on earth. So he strips the mask of megalomaniac pretense from Nebuchadnezzar and reveals to him the true depths of his inner weakness and helplessness. He breaks the man.

Of all forms of illness, psychotic breakdown is surely the most dreadful. The emotional pain of acute anxiety and depression seems far more crippling than any form of physical pain, and the prospect of losing one's mind is far more terrifying to many people than that of losing one's life. So it is a great comfort to learn from this passage that mental illness, like any form of illness, lies within the providential control of God. It is not necessarily demonic in origin, for sometimes God sends mental illness into people's lives, as he did to Nebuchadnezzar, to fulfill his chastening purpose. The writer to the Hebrews exhorts us: "Do not make light of the Lord's discipline, and do not lose heart when he rebukes you, because the Lord disciplines those he loves" (Heb 12:5-6, quoting Prov 3:11-12). For Nebuchadnezzar, mental illness was a form of divine discipline: a judgment on his pride, yes, but a judgment designed for correction, not mere retribution.

Over recent years, I have learned never to despise mentally ill people or to write them off as wrecks of humanity. God is often more real to those who experience mental illness than to those who have not. In that extremity of alienation and loneliness that only the insane experience, God can still communicate, human beings can still respond and spirituality can still grow. That reassurance is surely given to us by the example of Nebuchadnezzar here.

Act 3: The Lesson Nebuchadnezzar Learned

At the end of that time, I, Nebuchadnezzar, raised my eyes toward heaven, and my sanity was restored. Then I praised the Most High; I honored and glorified him who lives forever.
His dominion is an eternal dominion;
    his kingdom endures from generation to generation.
All the peoples of the earth
    are regarded as nothing.
He does as he pleases

> with the powers of heaven
> and the peoples of the earth.
> No one can hold back his hand
> or say to him: "What have you done?" (4:34-35)

It had taken the best part of a lifetime for Nebuchadnezzar to come to understand who God is, and poor Daniel must often have found himself doubting whether it would ever happen. But at last Nebuchadnezzar, king of Babylon, had come to terms with the fact that there was a Sovereign greater than he, a Sovereign who demanded not just religious toleration for those who, like Daniel and his friends, chose to follow him, but the personal submission of every human being on the face of the earth.

Nebuchadnezzar confessed that he was wrong when he said that great Babylon was built by his own power and for his own glory and majesty. The power and the glory he enjoyed were the gifts of a greater King. Nebuchadnezzar had no claim on his goodness. He knew that if God wanted to, God had only to speak the word and take away from him not only his kingdom but his very sanity. There was no ground of appeal if he did so choose to act. God was not accountable to anyone for his actions.

On the contrary, Nebuchadnezzar realized that he was accountable to God. He had refused to acknowledge it for years, preferring to maintain the pretense of his independence and the delusions of his pride. He thought God would be satisfied by faint praise. He thought God would not mind playing second fiddle to his ego. He thought he was strong enough to resist the claims of God's majesty on his life. But now he realized he was foolish even to try it.

> My sanity was restored, my honor and splendor were returned to me for the glory of my kingdom. My advisers and nobles sought me out, and I was restored to my throne and became even greater than before. Now I, Nebuchadnezzar, praise and exalt and glorify the King of heaven, because everything he does is right and all his ways are just. And those who walk in pride he is able to humble. (4:36-37)

Imagine the Jews listening to this story in exile. It is not hard to empathize with the excitement they must have felt. The power of God, they would have realized, is not to be measured by the power that his people wield in secular society. Here in Babylon they were politically disfranchised, territorially dispossessed, an exiled, marginalized people, swallowed up in a great pagan empire. But their God could still humble the most formidable of their pagan masters.

We, at the beginning of a new millennium, must learn the same lesson. We do not have to mourn the church's loss of worldly influence. We do not have to cry in desperation for immediate revival, as if all is lost when the people of God are not publicly honored in society and seen to be doing great things. We do not have to fear capture by a pluralist world. We do not need special political recognition. We do not need social privileges. Dare I say it as a Britisher, we do not need an established church. We need none of these things in order to claim the world for Jesus, for the kingdom we represent advances not by means of territorial annexation but by individual conversion. He can convert a Nebuchadnezzar, he can convert a Constantine, he can even convert my friend Robert.

In a world like ours, in which so many look into the mirror every morning and say, "I believe in myself" or "I can do it," this is a truth we need to lay hold of. Many people today are fully paid-up members of our secular humanist society with its supreme confidence in the unstoppable juggernaut of human progress and its exaggerated estimation of humanity's potential for achievement. Nineteenth-century poet Algernon Swinburne expressed it beautifully in that sarcastic mimicry of the song of the Christmas angels: "Glory to Man in the highest! for Man is the master of things."

But it is not so. If we have good brains, they are God's gift in creation; if we have opportunities to make money, they are his gifts in providence; if we have good looks, an athletic body or a special talent, they are all his sovereign gifts. We are not self-made people, as we pretend to be. "It is he who made us, and not we ourselves" (Ps 100:3, with footnote). Everything in our culture encourages self-promotion, self-assertion and self-reliance; every advertisement pushes the narcissistic image of the successful fellow or woman ever deeper into our subconscious. We flash our gold cards and sport our designer labels and caress our bodies with expensive fragrances. The only thing we lack is humility.

Let us learn from this testimony of a proud man. Self-sufficient he believed himself to be, but he was brought down by disaster and tragedy. God is not above using such experiences to shatter our confidence when we arrogantly boast of our ability to stand on our own two feet without his help: "Those who walk in pride he is able to humble." He can take away our health, our sanity, even our life itself. When we look in our mirror, then, what should we say? "Here is the greatness I have built by my mighty power and for my glory"? Rather, let us acknowledge that "by the grace of God I am what I am" (1 Cor 15:10). And if ever that confession starts to stick in our throats, we should remember Nebuchadnezzar.

Eight

Pride Goes Before a Fall

DANIEL 5

*T*wo vast and trunkless legs of stone
Stand in the desert. Near them, on the sand,
Half sunk, a shattered visage lies, whose frown
And wrinkled lip, and sneer of cold command,
Tell that its sculptor well those passions read. . . .
And on the pedestal these words appear:
"My name is Ozymandias, king of kings:
Look on my works, ye Mighty, and despair!"

The author of those well-known lines, Percy Bysshe Shelley, had a streak of anarchistic indignation in him that seethes beneath the tragic pathos of the scene he is describing. Who was this Ozymandias? That is Shelley's point, of course. No one has heard of him. For all his former glory, for all his pretentious titles, for all his megalomaniac claims, all that remains of Ozymandias is a pathetic broken colossus in a remote desert that nobody ever visits. The poem continues:

Nothing beside remains. Round the decay

Of that colossal wreck, boundless and bare,
The lone and level sands stretch far away.

The poet's unspoken verdict is clear. Thus may all the proud
conquerors of the earth meet their end: sunk in the oblivion of
ignominious desolation, the silence of the desert their only
epitaph.

The Rise and Fall of Belshazzar

Shelley would have liked the story of Belshazzar. In many respects
it conveys in narrative form the same contempt for proud tyrants,
the same judgment upon their arrogance, as his poem does. The
difference is that Ozymandias is, as far as I am aware, a figure of
Shelley's imagination, whereas Belshazzar of Babylon is most
definitely a figure of history.

How much time was left to Nebuchadnezzar after the events
of Daniel 4 we do not know, but it is clear that chapter 5 takes up
the story some years after his death. Archaeological studies have
been able to illumine the intervening years a little. We know that
following Nebuchadnezzar's death the power of Babylon de-
clined rapidly. The throne changed hands several times in quick
succession, probably as the result of violent coups by rival members of his dynasty. Eventually a noble called Nabonidus succeeded in establishing a measure of political stability, but not for
very long. There were internal squabbles within Babylon, and
previous vassal peoples took the opportunity to reassert their
independence.

To make matters worse, Nabonidus himself seems to have
been something of a religious crank. He abandoned the worship
of Marduk, the official religion of Babylon, and resurrected
instead the ancient cult of the moon god, Sin. Instead of pacify-
ing his fragile empire, he seems to have spent much of his time
excavating buried shrines and reviving forgotten rituals. Some
scholars believe that it was in pursuit of this strange religious
antiquarianism that in the latter years of his reign Nabonidus

deserted his capital city altogether and went to live in the Arabian desert. Others rather cynically suggest that he had seen the threat posed by Darius and decided he would be safer out of the firing line. Whatever his motives, the fact is that Nabonidus left the great metropolis of Babylon in the hands of his son Belshazzar.

At this point some may note that Daniel 5 says explicitly that Belshazzar's father was Nebuchadnezzar (5:2, 11, 13, 18). Some commentators, never reluctant to seize an opportunity to express their lack of confidence in Bible history, are quick to insist that the author of Daniel was lamentably ill-informed about the last days of Babylon; this, they say, is just one of many errors he made. But there is no need for such skepticism. Quite often in the Old Testament the word *father* is used in the loose sense of *ancestor* or *predecessor* (see NIV footnote here; also note how Elisha addresses Elijah as "My father!" in 2 Kings 2:12). This usage was particularly common in royal dynasties. Daniel 5 does not therefore necessarily imply that Belshazzar was genetically related to Nebuchadnezzar, although some scholars do believe he may have been his grandson.

Be that as it may, the key point as far as the story is concerned is that when at last the forces of Darius's new Medo-Persian empire swept south toward Babylon, it was the unfortunate Belshazzar who found himself seated on Nebuchadnezzar's throne. Slain "that very night" (5:30), Belshazzar, like Shelley's Ozymandias, faded into political oblivion, but without even a broken statue to commemorate him. Indeed, if it were not for Daniel 5 it is likely that most people would never have heard of him. It seems to me, though, that the narrator of Daniel, under the inspiration of the Holy Spirit, has recorded his story deliberately, as a contrast to the preceding account of Nebuchadnezzar in chapter 4. Often in biblical narrative there is a deliberate juxtaposition of two characters, inviting comparison. The narrator sets before us two proud tyrants, one who learned his lesson and one who did not.

The Man Who Tried to Forget

> King Belshazzar gave a great banquet for a thousand of his
> nobles and drank wine with them. While Belshazzar was drink-
> ing his wine, he gave orders to bring in the gold and silver
> goblets that Nebuchadnezzar his father had taken from the
> temple in Jerusalem, so that the king and his nobles, his wives
> and his concubines might drink from them. (5:1-2)

It is clear from the story's ending that the armies of Darius must
already have been closing in on Babylon at this time (5:30-31).
So this huge banquet must have been a rather pathetic attempt
on Belshazzar's part to brazen the situation out. Was he perhaps
worried about a preemptive coup on the part of some of his
nobles? Was this lavish hospitality designed to disarm any gathering hostility among them? Was it a piece of thinly disguised
escapism—"Let us eat, drink and be merry, for tomorrow we
die"? The narrator certainly seems keen to draw our attention to
the amount of alcohol that was flowing. He does not actually say
that the king was intoxicated, but there is a definite atmosphere
of debauchery about the proceedings. Contemporary readers of
this narrative would have recognized that it was in scandalous
breach of protocol in the Babylonian court that Belshazzar had
invited his royal harem to the party. It was a feast of wine, women
and (no doubt) song, a reckless orgy of self-indulgence, in
defiance of the imminent political emergency.

It is not clear what prompted Belshazzar to call for his normal
dinner service to be replaced by the sacred vessels that had been
confiscated from the temple in Jerusalem. Some suggest that it
was a drunken whim, but I suspect it was rather more calculated
than that.

Earlier I mentioned that Nabonidus, Belshazzar's father, was
a religious eccentric with a penchant for reviving outmoded
deities from Babylonia's polytheistic past. It is tempting to see
Belshazzar's actions here against the background of that current
imperial obsession. Did Belshazzar, for instance, superstitiously

attribute the failing fortunes of the Babylonian empire to Nebuchadnezzar's failure to venerate the ancient gods? Was this great banquet in fact a religious feast, a bacchanalian festival designed to propitiate those ancestral divinities that Babylon for too long had neglected?

If so, then the defilement of the temple vessels may well have been a public repudiation of Nebuchadnezzar's known sympathies for the cult of Yahweh practiced by the Jews, which Belshazzar quite probably regarded as an unpatriotic foible on Nebuchadnezzar's part. There can be little doubt, I think, that this is how the author of Daniel interprets it. The opening paragraph in chapter 5 stands in stark and deliberate contrast to the closing paragraph of chapter 4, where Nebuchadnezzar in humility confesses the supremacy of the God of the Jews. Here we find Belshazzar, in his arrogance, confessing his utter contempt for the God of the Jews.

> So they brought in the gold goblets that had been taken from
> the temple of God in Jerusalem, and the king and his nobles,
> his wives and his concubines drank from them. As they drank
> the wine, they praised the gods of gold and silver, of bronze,
> iron, wood and stone. (5:3-4)

The last sentence clearly suggests that this was a religious feast, or had religious implications. It was no drunken whim but rather a deliberate act of sacrilege, a desperate final attempt to invoke the powers of pagan deities in defiance of the so-called God of heaven whom Nebuchadnezzar had made so much of in his dotage.

It is not an unfamiliar scenario even today. Some years ago I met a minister's daughter who, some said, had had an excessively religious upbringing. If that was true she had certainly overreacted to it. Convinced that all her problems were the result of her Christian upbringing, she had engaged in a deliberate program of wild parties, drug abuse and promiscuous sex, as if the only way to liberate herself from the consequences of her repressive childhood was to spit in the eye of the God her parents worshiped. I met her when her cathartic fling had come to a sudden stop; she was in the hospital after an overdose, her mind a jumble of anxiety and guilt.

Perhaps it is no coincidence that Belshazzar's pagan revelry landed him in much the same state. This man who was so keen to display his public contempt for God was, we are told, at a stroke reduced to a blubbering heap of terror.

> Suddenly the fingers of a human hand appeared and wrote on the plaster of the wall, near the lampstand in the royal palace. The king watched the hand as it wrote. His face turned pale and he was so frightened that his knees knocked together and his legs gave way. (5:5-6)

We are meant to laugh. The narrator is deliberately playing up the comic aspect of this scene for the entertainment of his Jewish readers. There is an element of farce in his graphic description of Belshazzar's nervous collapse and a definite air of pantomime about the way in which, as so often in these stories, the wise men of Babylon are wheeled in, somewhat like the ubiquitous chorus in a Gilbert and Sullivan operetta.

> The king called out for the enchanters, astrologers and diviners to be brought and said to these wise men of Babylon, "Whoever reads this writing and tells me what it means will be clothed in purple and have a gold chain placed around his neck, and he will be made the third highest ruler in the kingdom."
>
> Then all the king's wise men came in, but they could not read the writing or tell the king what it meant. So King Belshazzar became even more terrified and his face grew more pale. His nobles were baffled. (5:7-9)

The deliberate parallel between this story and that of Nebuchadnezzar is clear. Once again, at a stroke, the king is reduced to terror; once again the science of Babylon proves impotent. One commentator likens this bevy of academics to the seemingly

inexhaustible company of analysts and experts whom newscast-
ers seem to summon almost instantaneously to comment on any
current event, no matter how unexpected or bizarre. Something
happens in the late morning and on the twelve o'clock news they
interview an expert about it. The analogy is quite a good one, I
think, and renders the speechlessness of these wise men all the
more startling because such experts are rarely stumped. They
can usually manage at least to bluff their way through. But these
royal advisers seem unable to offer any kind of response to the
king's inquiry.

In fact, the narrator seems to imply that they could not even
decipher the words the king had seen, let alone interpret them.
Why was this? Some have suggested that it was because the words
were written in an unknown script or because the letters were
jumbled in a cryptic fashion. I suspect that those few commentators are right who suggest a simpler explanation, namely that
the wise men could not read the writing because they could not
see it. There is nothing in the text to indicate that this ghostly
graffiti was visible to anybody but the king himself. Verse 9 tells
us that the king was terrified; everybody else was simply baffled.
If an apparition had appeared that was visible to all, then surely
everybody's knees would have been knocking, not just the king's.

Do you remember the story of the emperor's new clothes?
Because he believed he was wearing a fine new outfit, everybody
felt obliged to nod enthusiastically and pretend to see it too. But
privately they were whispering, "It's all in his mind, of course."
Perhaps the same kind of thing was going on here in the court
of Belshazzar. "He must have seen something in the shadows of
the lampstand just over there. It must be the stress of the
imminent Persian invasion or the effect of the booze. He has
been hitting the bottle a bit lately."

Only one person in the palace seems not to have been para-
lyzed by protocol in this way.

The queen, hearing the voices of the king and his nobles,

came into the banquet hall. "O king, live forever!" she said. "Don't be alarmed! Don't look so pale!" (5:10)

There is a great deal of interest among commentators regarding the precise identity of this royal lady. Although our translation calls her "queen," it seems clear from 5:2 that Belshazzar's wives were already present in the banquet hall, whereas this noble woman is recorded as entering the hall. Moreover, her bold entry into the king's presence, without invitation and with the bare minimum of conventional obsequiousness, proves that she must have possessed enormous personal prestige and authority. Many scholars therefore surmise that the word rendered "queen" should properly be translated "queen mother" (as the NIV footnote indicates). This figure is known to have frequently been accorded much more prestige in the ancient world than the king's escort.

Indeed, putting all the evidence together, it is far from impossible that this formidable matron was none other than the widow of Nebuchadnezzar himself. This would certainly explain the familiarity with court affairs of Nebuchadnezzar's day that she subsequently displays and also her tone of indignation and even rebuke at Belshazzar's disloyalty to the memory of his illustrious predecessor.

There is a man in your kingdom who has the spirit of the holy gods in him. In the time of your father [that is, your predecessor Nebuchadnezzar] he was found to have insight and intelligence and wisdom like that of the gods. King Nebuchadnezzar your father—your father the king, I say—appointed him chief of the magicians, enchanters, astrologers and diviners. This man Daniel, whom the king called Belteshazzar, was found to have a keen mind and knowledge and understanding, and also the ability to interpret dreams, explain riddles and solve difficult problems. Call for Daniel, and he will tell you what the writing means. (5:11-12)

The queen mother alone, perhaps, of all the nobles and royal advisers in the hall, recognizes that what Belshazzar has seen is no trick of the light, no alcohol-induced hallucination, but a divine vision, like those dreams that had had such a powerful influence on Nebuchadnezzar. There had been only one man in the kingdom who could interpret such visions. Mercifully, he was still alive, an old man by now, and no doubt discredited and pensioned off. For although he had once been a senior professor in the university, his monotheistic nonconformity was not likely to be tolerated in the current mood of pagan renaissance that Nabonidus and Belshazzar had instigated. Nevertheless, the king's anxiety is so desperate that he is willing to consult anything and anybody.

So Daniel was brought before the king, and the king said to him, "Are you Daniel, one of the exiles my father the king brought from Judah? I have heard that the spirit of the gods is in you and that you have insight, intelligence and outstanding wisdom. The wise men and enchanters were brought before me to read this writing and tell me what it means, but they could not explain it. Now I have heard that you are able to give interpretations and to solve difficult problems. If you can read this writing and tell me what it means, you will be clothed in purple and have a gold chain placed around your neck, and you will be made the third highest ruler in the kingdom." (5:13-16)

(Notice that little touch of authenticity: "the *third* highest ruler." The order would have been Nabonidus, Belshazzar, Daniel.)

Strange how quickly Belshazzar's contempt for the God of the Jews has evaporated! How can a man blasphemously defile God's temple one moment and shower extravagant honors on God's prophet the next? Such is the fickleness of a great deal of irreligion. A man may confidently toy with atheism and affirm that modern science has rendered it impossible to believe in the God of the Bible but still be outraged when the vicar refuses to hold a Christian funeral for his partner. A mother can play with mysticism, send her children to Halloween parties and express frightfully sophisticated opinions about the merits of New Age philosophy, but she is keen enough to ask for prayer when her children become psychiatrically disturbed as a result of occult dabbling. Again and again I have had my faith patronizingly dismissed as escapism, yet when there is big trouble—when Darius's troops are at the city walls, as it were—it is that same patronizing unbeliever who tries to escape (just as Belshazzar did, drowning his fears), and it is the believer who is able to help (as Daniel did).

The Man Who Never Learned

Then Daniel answered the king, "You may keep your gifts for yourself and give your rewards to someone else. Nevertheless, I will read the writing for the king and tell him what it means.

"O king, the Most High God gave your father Nebuchadnezzar sovereignty and greatness and glory and splendor. Because of the high position he gave him, all the peoples and nations and men of every language dreaded and feared him. Those the king wanted to put to death, he put to death; those he wanted to spare, he spared; those he wanted to promote, he promoted; and those he wanted to humble, he humbled. But when his heart became arrogant and hardened with pride, he was deposed from his royal throne and stripped of his glory. He was driven away from people and given the mind of an animal; he lived with the wild donkeys and ate grass like cattle; and his body was drenched with the dew of heaven, until he acknowledged that the Most High God is sovereign over the kingdoms of men and sets over them anyone he wishes.

"But you his son, O Belshazzar, have not humbled yourself, though you knew all this." (5:17-22)

Do you feel the drama the narrator so skillfully weaves into his account? He refers back to his previous story in which Nebuchadnezzar, inflated by his military success and narcissistic pride, succumbed to a devastating mental breakdown. Under the assault of his schizophrenic delusions he lived like a wild animal, out in the open. Yet in the midst of this insanity God was real to him and granted him remission, during which he published his encyclical. And, says Daniel, you, Belshazzar, knew all this. Nebuchadnezzar's encyclical was in the court records. These events were no myth circulating among the Jewish community. What happened to Nebuchadnezzar was on file, albeit hushed up. Belshazzar must have known about it because he was on the inside, with access to such privileged information. Almost certainly he was a young man in the court when it happened. It was common knowledge then. Belshazzar knew the extent of Nebuchadnezzar's power and how he had been humbled by the Most High God, confessing God's sovereignty over all human empires. Belshazzar was a petty little monarch by comparison, yet he thought he could defy the God who had humbled Nebuchadnezzar and get away with it.

> You . . . have not humbled yourself, though you knew all this. Instead, you have set yourself up against the Lord of heaven. You had the goblets from his temple brought to you, and you and your nobles, your wives and your concubines drank wine from them. You praised the gods of silver and gold, of bronze, iron, wood and stone, which cannot see or hear or understand. But you did not honor the God who holds in his hand your life and all your ways. Therefore he sent the hand that wrote the inscription. (5:22-24)

Once again we see why Daniel is rightly numbered among the prophets. Like Isaiah before Ahaz, with brilliant rhetoric he fearlessly denounces the blasphemous presumption of this pretentious monarch. But there is a major difference: Earlier prophets usually rebuked kings of Israel, whose culture was saturated with centuries of biblical heritage and who had the law of Moses on their bookshelf. But Daniel here is rebuking a king of Babylon, whose culture was bound up with centuries of pagan superstition and who had nothing on his bookshelf except the testimony of one converted illustrious predecessor. Yet, insists Daniel, it should have been enough. Belshazzar should have known better than to challenge the majesty of the Most High God by such a calculated act of sacrilege. God might have overlooked a sin of ignorance, but these defiled vessels scattered around the drink-sodden banquet hall represent a flagrant and deliberate act of contempt. Like Pharaoh before Moses, Belshazzar has waved his fist at God ("Who is the LORD, that I should obey him?" [Ex 5:2]), and like Pharaoh he will pay the price for his hardened arrogance. This man who tried to forget has become a frightened man, and the man who would not learn will now become a condemned man as he hears Daniel's interpretation of the writing on the wall:

This is the inscription that was written:

MENE, MENE, TEKEL, PARSIN

This is what these words mean:

Mene: God has numbered the days of your reign and brought it to an end.

Tekel: You have been weighed on the scales and found wanting.

Peres: Your kingdom is divided and given to the Medes and Persians. (5:25-28)

Scholars have puzzled over these words in the vision, but it seems clear now that each of these three words is in fact the name of a small weight, such as would have been used as currency in the marketplace. The underlying thought, then, is that of being weighed in the balance of divine justice. Daniel, in keeping with the proverbial style of a Middle Eastern sage, has woven a pun around each of these words, linking the Aramaic noun to a similar-sounding verb in order to reinforce the theme of being weighed in the balances and found wanting. *Mene,* the first little weight, means "mina" or "numbered": God has numbered Belshazzar's days and found that he has reached his credit limit. *Tekel* can mean "shekel" or "weighed": God has weighed Belshazzar's life and found it light on goodness. *Parsin,* the plural of *peres,* denotes half-shekels or half-minas. This means two things for Belshazzar: first "divided," which is what his kingdom is going to be, and second "Persia," for God has appointed Belshazzar's executioner. Like the tolling of enormous bells, Daniel rings out the king's death knell.

Still, it seems, Belshazzar tries to pretend that all is well. He forces his promised goodies upon the reluctant Daniel:

Then at Belshazzar's command, Daniel was clothed in purple, a gold chain was placed around his neck, and he was proclaimed the third highest ruler in the kingdom. (5:29)

Although Daniel had told him that he did not want any of these things, it is as if the king is trying to convince himself, and the many nobles present, that Daniel's oracle was an encouraging one! But the writing was on the wall, as we say, indelibly inscribed by the hand of God. The moving finger had written, and no eleventh-hour compliments paid to the preacher were going to cancel the funeral.

That very night Belshazzar, king of the Babylonians, was slain, and Darius the Mede took over the kingdom. (5:30)

The narrator's lesson is clear. We human beings are accountable to God. This is his constant theme. We saw it in the story of Daniel in the lions' den, which follows in Daniel 6. God made us, and by his grace we enjoy whatever power and privilege are ours. He does not tell us when we shall be called to give account, but for every one of us, no matter how mighty we are, that day will come:

The boast of heraldry, the pomp of power,

And all that beauty, all that wealth e'er gave,

Awaits alike the inevitable hour,

The paths of glory lead but to the grave.

(from Thomas Gray's *Elegy Written in a Country Churchyard*)

Encouragement or Challenge?

Nebuchadnezzar had learned that lesson in time, but Belshazzar did not. The question the narrator is subtly putting to us as we read this story is: Have *we* learned it? For those who have, the story of Belshazzar is recorded for our comfort and encouragement; for those who have not, for our challenge and mourning.

As we have seen before, the Jews who read this book in the years after the exile needed reassurance in a hostile world where titanic forces of one pagan empire after another dominated their horizon. They desperately needed to know that no matter how formidable their tyrant, God would have the last word. The writing was on the wall, not just for Belshazzar but for every heathen despot who thought he could trample with impunity over the sensitivities of the people of God.

The same lesson is not without relevance to the church at the beginning of the twenty-first century. We too, like the Jews in exile, are increasingly reduced to little more than a minority sect in a world where secularism is calling all the shots. Christianity is lampooned by television comedians and marginalized in the corridors of power. Like Daniel, many a Christian feels isolated, a lone voice at college, on the factory floor, in the office, in the classroom, among neighbors—even in the family these days. We need to be reassured. The writing is on the wall. God will have the last word, so we must not be afraid, like Daniel, to tell the truth to those who, like Belshazzar, do not know the sovereign God or acknowledge that their lives are in his hand.

It may be that "Truth [is] forever on the scaffold, Wrong forever on the throne," as Lowell wrote, but it is also true that "that scaffold sways the future, and, behind the dim unknown, / Standeth God within the shadow, keeping watch above his own." That is the message of Daniel, a message we shall see repeated when we think about Daniel's vision of the future in our next chapter. We must not miss the irony in the fact that Belshazzar is replaced by the Medo-Persian empire, which, as every Jew knew, permitted their return to the Promised Land. In the fall of this cruel tyrant, then, God is showing his sovereign control over circumstances as he establishes another king through whom the prayers of the saints will be answered.

That brings me to the other purpose for which this story was written down. It was recorded not just to comfort and reassure the believer but also to discomfort the unbeliever. The book of Daniel is unique in the Old Testament in that although it begins and ends in the Hebrew language, all the stories from chapter 2 to chapter 6 are written in Aramaic. Why is this? Scholars have proposed many explanations, but I will state mine: I believe that this book was not written for the Jewish community alone. Much of it, I believe, was published as evangelistic tracts for the Persians. Aramaic was the lingua franca of the Persian empire, which was about to envelope Babylonia. The author of Daniel, therefore, used Aramaic for the same reason the New Testament apostles used Greek: his aim was not only to encourage God's people but to convert Gentiles, so he wanted everybody to understand what he wrote.

Daniel had great confidence in his God. A God who can convert a Nebuchadnezzar and use a Darius is a God who can convert anybody, Jew or Gentile. At this critical time in their history we are beginning to see the emergence of a universalist vision among the Jewish people: something that would pave the way for the kingdom of God as Jesus would preach it, a kingdom that was open to all.

These stories therefore challenge the obdurate pride of sinners. It is the intention of the Holy Spirit, through this story of Belshazzar, to convert men and women. The writing is on the wall for them. God has numbered their days, they are weighed in the balance, and their period of self-rule is coming to an end. It is only a matter of time before the God who holds their life in his hands will call them to account. Perhaps they are trying to forget the inexorable approach of that day—drowning their fears in alcohol, like Belshazzar. Many do run away into the frenetic pursuit of pleasure or money or sex—anything rather than face up to the God upon whom we depend for the very breath of our lives.

Could it be that we have forgotten that we hold our lives on divine loan? Could it be that, like Belshazzar defiling the temple vessels, we have dedicated that which belongs to a holy God to the profane idols of our own self-indulgence? Do we not see what a blasphemous sacrilege it is to defile our lives in such a way? These questions must be pressed home to the non-Christian. For there will certainly come a time, as for Belshazzar, when even as we try to escape we are brought up short. A bereavement, a broken relationship, illness, redundancy, an accident: God uses many tactics to break through our spiritual amnesia. But not one of us can succeed in evading him forever.

Have we learned the lesson from which Nebuchadnezzar profited but that Belshazzar refused to learn? We cannot plead ignorance any more than he could. All he had was the testimony of Nebuchadnezzar's encyclical. We have Bibles, books, preachers, teachers and Christian testimonies by the score. The Most High is sovereign over the kingdoms on earth, and he holds our lives in his hands. What if he should weigh those lives today?

"My name is Ozymandias, king of kings:
Look on my works, ye Mighty, and despair!"
Nothing beside remains. Round the decay
Of that colossal wreck, boundless and bare
The lone and level sands stretch far away.

Shelley is right: the world is littered with the broken relics of once-great emperors who thought to master the world, reduced to trunkless legs of stone in the desert. Genghis Khan, Alexander, Julius Caesar, Napoleon, Stalin, Chairman Mao: look on your works, and despair! Did you not learn the lesson either? Your name is not "king of kings." That title belongs to another. His memorial is not a ruined statue but an empty cross, and he is not moldering in some lost tomb but is risen and glorified. From his throne this King of kings and Lord of lords reaches down to us and offers forgiveness for the past and hope for the future. Learn the lesson Belshazzar refused to learn, for the writing is on the wall: "Pride goes before destruction, a haughty spirit before a fall" (Prov 16:18).

There is a better success, a nobler dignity, a higher glory, than those that are sought by people who pride themselves on their power and achievements. "Let the same mind be in you," it says, "that was in Christ Jesus, who, though he was in the form of God, did not regard equality with God as something to be exploited, but emptied himself, taking the form of a slave." If ever anyone had the right to be proud, it was he. He had come from God, he was going to God, he *was* God. But, continues the apostle, "he humbled himself" (Phil 2:5-8 NRSV). This mind is the only sane mind. To indulge in narcissistic obsession with the image of our own inflated egos is to invite disaster. Let this mind be in you that was in Christ Jesus.

Nine

A Future &
a Hope

DANIEL 2

*D*avid Cook tells a story about an undergraduate who was
writing home at the end of a semester. The letter goes something like this:

> I know you haven't heard much from me in recent months, but
> the fact is this. A few weeks back, there was a fire in the flat and
> I lost all my possessions. In fact I only escaped with my life by
> jumping out of a second-floor window. In the process of doing
> so I broke my leg, so I ended up in the hospital. Fortunately, I
> met the most wonderful nurse there. We immediately fell in love,
> and, well, to cut a long story short, last Saturday we got married.
> Many of our friends say this was too hasty, but I am convinced
> that our love will more than compensate for the difference
> between our social backgrounds and ethnic origins.
>
> By this time, Mum and Dad, I suspect you may be getting a
> bit worried, so let me tell you straight away that everything I
> have written in this letter up to now is false. I made it up. The
> truth is, two weeks ago I failed my final exams. I just want you

to get this in the proper perspective.

A proper perspective on their misfortunes is what the Jews in exile needed too, and it was the task of prophets like Ezekiel and Daniel to provide it. We have seen how Ezekiel, in the early chapters of his prophecy, provided the exiles with a theological interpretation of their experience. They had suffered this national humiliation of exile as a divine judgment on their idolatrous apostasy. But God had not deserted them; on the contrary, he had accompanied them into exile and still had a purpose for them in spite of it. We saw how relevant all this is to a church that is compromised and secularized in pagan society, in need of words of rebuke and judgment.

We also have looked at the early chapters of the book of Daniel and seen how he provided the exiles with a personal model of how they could continue to practice the distinctive biblical faith and maintain biblical holiness in the midst of the pagan environment in which they found themselves. He even demonstrated that it was possible to win notable converts and exert considerable influence among secular rulers by means of such courageous testimony. Again we saw the relevance of that for Christians facing the prospect of becoming a minority group in a pagan society once more.

Faith in the Future

In their different ways Ezekiel and Daniel have enabled the exiles to get their situation into perspective and to be positive about their predicament. But there remains a further strategy that both Ezekiel and Daniel have in common in this regard. It dominates the closing chapters of both books and can be expressed in a nutshell like this: faith cannot survive in a pagan world unless it has great confidence in the final triumph of God. Without a future perspective we cannot survive as Christians in a pagan society.

This too is of great relevance to our contemporary society. People at the beginning of the twenty-first century have lost confidence in the future. Optimism about the destiny of the human race has almost totally collapsed today. The vision of utopia that fired so much political idealism in the nineteenth century lies wrecked under the carnage of wars and revolutions of unprecedented scale and savagery; the predictions of human progress led by technological advance lie shrouded in the mushroom cloud of Hiroshima and the pollution of Chernobyl. Though there may still be a few who cling to the old dreams of a man-made paradise on earth, the vast majority of people dare to view the world realistically rather than through the rose-tinted glasses of a discredited humanism. For them, such spurious visions are just the secularized equivalent of those false prophets who in Ezekiel's day cried "Peace" when there was no peace (Ezek 13:10). Sir Kenneth Clark, in his celebrated book *Civilization,* wrote, "Confident articles on the future are to my mind the most disreputable of all public utterances."

As the mystical year 2000 approaches, global insecurity about the future becomes more and more acute. One young American student put it to me like this: "We used to trust the generals, but Vietnam changed all that. We used to trust the politicians, but Watergate changed all that. We used to trust the scientists, but Three Mile Island changed all that. Now there's nobody left to trust."

It would have been all too easy for the exiles to lapse into the same kind of disillusionment. Everybody had let them down too: their governments, their armies, even their religion. What hope did they have in exile? How could they possibly sing the Lord's song in that strange land? It is perhaps the greatest triumph of the exilic prophets that hope did survive. It survived largely because these prophets, under the inspiration of God, discovered eschatology, a theology of the future. The failure of the past, instead of destroying the hope of those exiled Jews, refashioned it. The failure of the kingdom of David to fulfill their great expectations was paradoxically the catalyst that gave rise to a new messianic expectation of the kingdom of God.

A Vision of the Future

We catch a glimpse of this in Nebuchadnezzar's great vision, which Daniel interpreted for him. The king had dreamed but could remember only his restlessness, not the dream's content. The sages could not tell him what it was, but, after prayer, Daniel was able to give him both the content and the interpretation.

> You looked, O king, and there before you stood a large statue—an enormous, dazzling statue, awesome in appearance. The head of the statue was made of pure gold, its chest and arms of silver, its belly and thighs of bronze, its legs of iron, its feet partly of iron and partly of baked clay. While you were watching, a rock was cut out, but not by human hands. It struck the statue on its feet of iron and clay and smashed them. Then the iron, the clay, the bronze, the silver and the gold were broken to pieces at the same time and became like chaff on a threshing floor in the summer. The wind swept them away without leaving a trace. But the rock that struck the statue became a huge mountain and filled the whole earth. (2:31-35)

This dream of a colossus, vulnerable at its feet, that is supernaturally pulverized and replaced by a huge mountain is not something that should surprise us in a person like Nebuchadnezzar. As I surmised in chapter seven, a psychiatrist might well speculate that such a dream was precipitated by personal insecurity. In his megalomaniac ambition, Nebuchadnezzar had sought to make himself into an impregnable giant, towering over the world like one of those many statues of deity that adorned his new city of Babylon. But his dream brings to the surface his subconscious doubts about the strength of his edifice. He anticipates the destruction of his empire and of himself with it. Such a dream would indeed be a glimpse of the future, the future that Nebuchadnezzar in his arrogance was constructing for himself.

But Daniel is convinced that there is more to this dream than that. This is not merely the emperor's repressed subconscious confronting him with his unspoken fears, though God may have used that to generate this dream. In this dream God has actually broken in to provide Daniel with a singular opportunity to influence this pagan empire to which he had been brought, and to set its dominion in the context of God's greater purpose for his people. That is how he goes on to interpret the dream.

> This was the dream, and now we will interpret it to the king. You, O king, are the king of kings. The God of heaven has given you dominion and power and might and glory; in your hands he has placed mankind and the beasts of the field and the birds of the air. Wherever they live, he has made you ruler over them all. You are that head of gold.
>
> After you, another kingdom will arise, inferior to yours. Next, a third kingdom, one of bronze, will rule over the whole earth. Finally, there will be a fourth kingdom, strong as iron— for iron breaks and smashes everything—and as iron breaks things to pieces, so it will crush and break all the others. Just as you saw that the feet and toes were partly of baked clay and partly of iron, so this will be a divided kingdom; yet it will have some of the strength of iron in it, even as you saw iron mixed with clay. As the toes were partly iron and partly clay, so this kingdom will be partly strong and partly brittle. And just as you saw the iron mixed with baked clay, so the people will be a mixture and will not remain united, any more than iron mixes with clay. (2:36-43)

Down through history, Jews and Christians have been keen to identify in historical terms the four kingdoms represented by the strata in Nebuchadnezzar's statue. Unfortunately, there is no consensus. Much depends upon one's view of the authorship of the book of Daniel and the interpretation of its later chapters. Suffice it to say that the head of gold, as we are told quite clearly, represents the Babylonian empire. There is no doubt about that. Opinions differ, however, about the legs of iron. Some hold that they represent the Greek empire of Alexander the Great, which was divided at his death (hence the iron-and-clay instability of the feet). Others hold that this fourth empire of iron and clay represents the Roman empire of the Caesars. One's view of the iron empire dictates the identification of the silver and the bronze empires. In the first hypothesis (iron = Greece), the silver is the Median empire and the bronze the Persian. In the second hypothesis (iron = Rome), the silver is the Persian empire and the bronze the Greek. So the order is either Babylon, Media, Persia, Greece, or Babylon, Persia, Greece, Rome.

The Greek option has generally been preferred by liberal scholars, but is defended by some notable evangelicals such as John Goldingay. The main argument in favor of it is that the latter chapters of Daniel, which in many ways build on this vision and expand it, are quite definitely preoccupied with the crises that befell the Jews in the time of the Maccabees, during the Greek period, in the second century B.C. It is generally true that prophetic books in the Bible address a particular period of time, often close to the author, and for that reason liberals take the view that the book of Daniel is in fact a second-century work, composed under the pseudonym Daniel for the encouragement of Jews in the Maccabean period. Most evangelicals would discount that position as unnecessarily skeptical regarding the ability of inspired writers to predict the future in detail. Even if we do so, however, there is no denying that the latter chapters of the book do seem to anticipate the arrival of the kingdom of God in the immediate wake of the fall of Antiochus Epiphanes in the Maccabean period. There is little in the later part of the book that could be identified as a prophetic anticipation of the Roman Empire, whereas the references to the Greek period are extremely obvious.

The Roman option is the traditional conservative view and is well illustrated by the classic commentary of E. J. Young. The main arguments in favor of it are twofold. First, the Median empire, which has to be included in the list of four if one takes the Greek view, was scarcely an empire. It was more of a transition period between the Babylonian and the Persian empires. Second, and perhaps more important for conservative readers, Jesus himself seems to make the identification with the Roman period when he implies that "the abomination that causes desolation," spoken of by Daniel, still awaited fulfillment in his day (Mt 24:15). Most would see this as a reference to the desecration of the temple by the Roman army at the time of the destruction of Jerusalem in A.D. 70.

It is impossible to do justice to the debate between these two points of view within the constraints of this chapter. Could it be that Scripture deliberately makes it difficult to identify the fourth kingdom with certainty because it has an interest in keeping the details of the end of the world vague? Could it be that Scripture wants us always to regard eschatology as relevant to the reader's own generation, whatever that may be, and that therefore we ought not to expect detailed forecasts that can be specifically tied down to particular periods in history? Could it be that Scripture wants to discourage us from trying to work out countdowns to the end of the world?

Nailing the Future

The book of Daniel has certainly been a happy hunting ground for all kinds of prognostications, dispensationalist wall charts, slide rule calculations and so on. There are some who can barely read the latest newspaper headline without rushing to the book of Daniel to find the event anticipated there. Whenever there is conflict in the Middle East, particularly Babylon, or Iraq as it now is, the opportunities are irresistible!

Surely such speculation cannot be right. When the disciples asked Jesus, "What will be the sign of your coming and of the end of the age?" Jesus immediately replied, "Watch out that no one deceives you" (Mt 24:3-4). They wanted the details, but all he wanted to say, in this matter of interpreting the signs of the end, was that people are easily led astray and soon jump to false conclusions. I would suggest that he proceeds to illustrate the sort of false conclusion he means by the way he goes on to instruct his disciples: "You will hear of wars and rumors of wars," he tells them (24:6).

You can almost see the disciples rubbing their hands together with glee. "Oh good, that's one sign we can watch out for: wars and rumors of wars. Good."

"See to it that you are not alarmed," Jesus continues. "Such things must happen, but the end is still to come" (24:6). Picture the crestfallen disappointment on those poor disciples' faces as they cross that sign off their list!

He continues, "There will be famines and earthquakes in various places." Ah! Another sign! "All these are the beginning of birth pains," he says (24:7-8).

When we see these "signs of the end," as they are fancifully called, the temptation will always be to assume that "this is it." Indeed, that is precisely what has happened down through history. During periods of wars, famines, earthquakes or whatever, there has always been a ready market for adventist hysteria. Sometimes the mere date on the calendar can produce that kind of urgency. There was widespread millennialist hysteria around the turn of the first millennium. It is no surprise that as we approach the year 2000, Christians are again focusing on the imminence of the Second Coming and talking about the restoration of all things before Jesus' return. But whenever these events have happened in the past, the crisis has gone by and the situation has stabilized. Those disasters thought to be so severe that they must be a prelude to the end of the world, those dates thought to herald Christ's return, have proved to portend no such thing. The end is not yet; these are just the beginning of birth pains.

We are always on the edge of the end times. The Jews were right to feel that the kingdom of God was imminent in the second century B.C. The apostles were right to feel that it was imminent in the first century A.D. The Levellers in the days of Cromwell were right to think it was about to come then, in the seventeenth century, and believers today are right to believe that it is imminent now. Where we go wrong is in thinking we know with certainty that "this is it," gambling everything on that speculation. The Master himself told us that we cannot know the date or the time. He himself did not know. What matters is that we should be ready at all times.

There is no point, therefore, in anxiously trying to crack the later chapters of Daniel. That is to miss their main lesson, which is that the kingdom of God is coming and that it is always imminent. There is a tension between the "now" and the "not yet," which we have to hold on to. What Nebuchadnezzar's statue portrays for us, for instance, is surely a picture of increasing decadence in the human race. The kingdoms of the world become progressively less noble, more fragile and more divided as time goes by. No doubt that would have meant something special for the Jews in the Maccabean period as Alexander's empire fragmented. No doubt it meant something special to those who lived under the Roman Empire. No doubt it means something special in our day. But we are not to make naive identifications: "this equals that." All we can say is that as time goes by the vaunted ambitions of human empire will be found to have feet of clay; the optimistic dreams of our man-made utopias will again and again end in disillusionment.

Fearful of the Future

This message is of enormous relevance to turn-of-the-millennium people because that is exactly how we feel about events. We are scared of the future because what we thought was going to carry us forward in triumph has proved unstable and vulnerable. This generates great anxiety because the future seems to be coming so fast. Mark Twain told a class of schoolchildren at the end of the nineteenth century: "Methuselah lived to be 969 years old, but you boys and girls will see more changes in the next fifty years than Methuselah saw in his entire lifetime." Of course, his prediction has been absolutely right. Anybody over fifty has seen extraordinary changes take place. If the same rate of change continues in the next fifty years, can we imagine what the world will be like? It is a frightening thought.

Carl Jung warned the Western world: "We have plunged down a cataract of progress which sweeps us into the future with ever wilder violence the further it takes us from our roots." Alvin Toffler, in his seminal book *Future Shock*, took his cue from those words and spelled out what the pace of change is doing to the human psyche in our day: "Our galloping technology introduces change so rapidly that human beings experience a dizzying disorientation. We rocket society into an environment so ephemeral, so unfamiliar, as to threaten millions with a massive adaptational breakdown."

I suppose it has always been true that as we get older we feel less and less in tune with modern ways. We talk about the good old days when things were much better than they are now. But it is noticeable that this sense of alienation from the present is setting in earlier and earlier. People used to start feeling nostalgic in their sixties; now they start in their thirties. Even teenagers are becoming unusually interested in the music and culture of earlier decades, as if they too want to haul back on the reins of time and slow down its headlong charge. They want space to enjoy one cultural phase before moving on to the next. It is the uncertainty of all this sudden change that disturbs us. We human beings need a secure environment, but we wonder if the changes we will encounter in our lifetime will be of such magnitude that we will be unable to cope with them.

There are plenty of predictions and forecasts, of course, made by everybody from science fiction authors to government think-tanks. Will the greenhouse effect melt the polar icecap so that we have to retreat before rising sea levels? Will the hole in the ozone layer expand and lead to widespread deaths from skin cancer? Will Saddam Hussein fire his nuclear missiles and blow us all up? Arthur C. Clarke, author of *2001: A Space Odyssey*, is reputed to have once observed, "No age has shown more interest in the future than our age—which is ironic, since we may not have one." The question of human destiny is pressing ever more urgently upon consciousness at the turn of the century. Where is this remorseless river of time, which every year seems to flow faster and faster, taking us?

These feelings about the future generate not only great anxiety but also profound apathy. A century ago the humanists were hailing evolution as the guarantor of a wonderful future for the human race. Marx even believed that a paradise of harmony and prosperity was within the grasp of his generation, because revolution could precipitate the inevitable results of historical evolution into the present. Today such optimistic ideas sound hollow, almost laughable. Experience has shown them to be fantasies of an infantile political imagination, as far removed from reality as Disneyland from Hiroshima. We have completely lost faith in utopia.

That disillusionment has its tragic side. One does not have to mourn the fact that the intoxicated expectations of early socialists have been sobered by a few bucketfuls of cold political pragmatism. It does not seriously sadden me that people are becoming wary of scientific advance. But it does worry me that in losing their dream of utopia, people have lost the vision that gave meaning to human existence. Whatever the evolutionists say, mere survival is not enough for human beings. What is the purpose of our survival? Without a vision for the future, human beings will never be inspired to use their creative potential to the full. Rather, they languish in apathy and are dangerously near to despair. We see the signs of that apathy in people's almost neurotic defenses against anxiety; they shut the future out with a kind of myopic self-indulgence. The philosophy that says "Enjoy yourself while you can" is becoming ever more characteristic of our culture.

Slowly but surely, such pessimism about the future tears the guts out of a culture. People have nothing to work for, nothing to save for and nothing to live for beyond their immediate desire. We are a consumer society, demanding instant gratification and unwilling to wait till we can afford it (a mentality with consequences for the whole economy, it can be argued, as we saddle ourselves with loans and credit card debts). Like sailors without a compass, we are letting the wind of our desires steer us where it will, making the best of things now, regardless of where we might be heading. A cavalier enthusiasm for progress, irrespective of any clear sense of direction, is what characterizes our world. The trouble is that our boat is powered by an engine of technological expertise, which generates a level of propulsion inconceivable before, yet we have lost interest in the compass and the rudder.

What our world needs is a dream of the future. Politics has largely lost its dreams. People talk not so much of bureaucracy as of *adhocracy:* if it works for the moment, let's do it. That is the general philosophy. Wider questions about the kind of society we want to create, the social evils we want to eliminate, the political goals we want to achieve—these we have lost interest in. Keep the ship afloat: that's the rule. We do not need the compass and the rudder, because we do not know where we want to go. Dreams of human destiny, we have learned, let us down.

Richard Crossman, in a Fabian lecture of 1950, confessed the failure of the socialist dream in candid terms: "All the obvious things have been done which we fought for and argued about, and yet mysteriously . . . the ideal . . . has not been achieved. We have created the means for the good life which they all laid down and said, 'If you do all these things, after that there'll be a classless society.' Well, there isn't." And what British socialism discovered in the 1950s, Eastern Bloc socialism discovered in the 1980s.

Christina Rossetti describes this kind of disillusionment in a lovely poem called "Mirage":

The hope I dreamed of was a dream,
Was but a dream, and now I awake,

Exceeding comfortless, and worn, and old,
For dreams' sake.

Hope for the Future

Our culture longs for a dream, not a mirage; a prophecy, not a fantasy. That is something that the Christian church distinctively can provide for our age. Our trump card, if you like, is our vision of the future. There never has been a time when eschatology was more important. Down through the centuries the people of God have always had a theology of hope. Ezekiel's visions enabled the exiles to survive their Babylonian captivity. It was through that theology of hope as conveyed by the book of Daniel that the faithful Jews survived as believers in the days of the Maccabees and Antiochus Epiphanes' persecution in the second century B.C. It was that theology of hope, as filled out in the gospel of the kingdom, that gave the early church the courage to persevere under Roman persecution in the first century A.D.

Perhaps one of the greatest examples of the importance of this theology of hope can be seen in the collapse of the Roman Empire in the fifth century A.D. In 410, Augustine, bishop of Hippo in North Africa, heard the news that Rome had been sacked. I doubt whether we today can imagine how devastating this news was. It was even more devastating than the fall of Jerusalem, for Rome was the center of the whole universe. Rome represented civilization. For centuries this great city had dominated the Mediterranean, yet it had fallen to a violent and heretical Gothic king.

On the day the news arrived Augustine preached a sermon. He compared the sack of Rome to the destruction of Sodom and told his congregation not to lose heart: "There will be an end to every earthly kingdom, for this world is passing away. This world is but a breath. But do not fear. Your youth shall be renewed as an eagle." It is significant that he took up those words of comfort addressed to the exiles under Babylonian captivity: "Those who hope in the LORD . . . will soar on wings like eagles" (Is 40:31). Augustine spent much of the rest of his life writing his great book on the city that, unlike Rome, can never pass away, *The City of God.*

This biblical theology of hope was important eleven centuries later for the Huguenot Protestants suffering in France. Calvin's great commentary on Daniel was written specifically for them, for he felt that it was profoundly relevant to their situation. "Whatever was predicted of the changing and vanishing splendors of the ancient monarchies and the perpetual existence of Christ's kingdom is in these days no less useful to us," he says, commenting on Daniel 2. "God has shown how all earthly powers must fail, and those kings whose sway is the most extended shall find by sorrowful experience how horrible a judgment will fall upon them unless they willingly submit to the sovereign sway of Christ."

Calvin's great theme in his interpretation of Daniel is that God must win. Because of this, Christians should stand out like beacons in our contemporary world. It is not just that we maintain habits of religious worship in a secular age or that we uphold standards of moral behavior in a permissive society. What ought to be the most obvious thing about Christians today is our positive attitude toward the future in the midst of a society that is growing increasingly pessimistic, despondent, anxious, apathetic and directionless. Jesus said that in the last days "nations will be in anguish and perplexity. . . . Men will faint from terror, apprehensive of what is coming on the world, for the heavenly bodies will be shaken" (Lk 21:25-26). There will be no security anywhere. But when these things happen, he said, his followers would be the only people standing up. They would be visible. They would be the only people lifting up their heads, knowing that their redemption was drawing near.

Christians are people of hope, and in these days in which we live, hope marks us out more dramatically, perhaps, than anything else.

Ten

New Life for God's People

EZEKIEL 37

*I*n the last chapter we caught a glimpse of the Bible's vision for the end of the age. In this chapter I want to reflect on a nearer hope, specifically the hope of revival in the church.

Such is the hunger of human beings for hope and purpose that they have always dreamed of a new and better world just around the corner. Plato called it the Republic. Thomas More called it Utopia. Karl Marx called it the classless society. At the beginning of the twenty-first century we are seeing the rise of a new secular eschatology, as New Age philosophy looks forward to the Age of Aquarius. This is the secular alternative to true biblical hope for the future. It is a message that offers hope without judgment. And insofar as some Christian teachers today preach hope without warning of judgment, they are playing into its hands.

The Beginning of Hope
It is only after years of preaching judgment that Ezekiel, in his final chapters, begins to speak of hope. The transition is marked

by an event the date of which is sealed into Ezekiel's mind: "In the twelfth year of our exile, in the tenth month on the fifth day, a man who had escaped from Jerusalem came to me and said, 'The city has fallen!'" (33:21).

The Jews of Ezekiel's day had taken a long while to reach a pitch of despair. They enjoyed an extraordinarily vigorous hope, even in the years after the first deportation. For in spite of their political insignificance, and in spite of the fact that they had been beaten by the Babylonians, while Jerusalem survived false prophecy survived, and with it false hope. *It will only be a matter of time,* they thought, *before we are back. Whatever catastrophe may overtake our neighbors, we shall be safe. The temple is inviolable. Jerusalem is the city of God; it cannot be taken.* Right up to the end Judah retained its confidence in these things. Only when that confidence was shattered could God bring the nation to that pitch of despair beyond which true hope was possible.

Ezekiel, true prophet that he was, could see that. He had been predicting the fall of Jerusalem for years; he had preached it, dramatized it, allegorized it and used a host of bizarre and eccentric devices to prepare his fellow exiles for the moment when they would hear this tragic news. Now at last his words had proved true. The unimaginable had happened. The center of the Jewish national dream was no more. The last thread of Israel's tattered pride had snapped.

When the news arrived, Ezekiel records, "my mouth was opened" (33:22). And what did he say? "I told you so"? No. He proved himself a true pastor. The people had accepted the word of judgment and were devastated by it. So now he was released, almost overnight, to become a prophet of hope for them. We then find in all the subsequent chapters of Ezekiel prophecies of hope.

It is interesting that the first dimension of this new hope he glimpsed was a new and better leadership for God's people. That is the thrust of chapter 34. The monarchy of Israel had been responsible for so much of the nation's apostasy. Israel's rulers simply had not cared for the flock as they should have done. But Ezekiel, as his mind began to probe the future, realized that God would one day raise up a new king of the lineage of David, one who, with strength and compassion, would lead the people of God into an era of unparalleled prosperity and security. "I will place over them one shepherd, my servant David. . . . I the LORD will be their God, and my servant David will be prince among them" (34:23-24). Notice the double fulfillment of these words in subsequent history. After the return from exile, Zerubbabel, of the Davidic line, was made governor; but Christians know that the real king Ezekiel was talking about is Jesus, the Messiah.

The other major dimension of Ezekiel's hope, and the one I want to focus on in this chapter, is his emphasis on the renewal of the people themselves.

The first step in this, Ezekiel says, was to be forgiveness for the past. "I will sprinkle clean water on you, and you will be clean; I will cleanse you from all your impurities and from all your idols" (36:25). In a sense, of course, this was nothing new, because God had pardoned his people on many occasions in the past. Yet that had not solved the fundamental problem of their ongoing sinfulness. If this future utopia that Ezekiel longed for was going to be permanent and impregnable, something more was needed than simply to be forgiven. Ezekiel anticipates that with extraordinary prophetic insight in the subsequent verse: "I will give you a new heart and put a new spirit in you; I will remove from you your heart of stone and give you a heart of flesh" (36:26).

In New Testament vocabulary, this spiritual heart transplant is called regeneration. "I tell you the truth," Jesus says to Nicodemus, "no one can see the kingdom of God unless he is born again" (Jn 3:3). Ezekiel agrees. Jesus may even have had this very passage in mind when he spoke to Nicodemus. There can be no kingdom of God, then, until this root of moral rebelliousness in the human heart is eradicated by the indwelling Spirit of God.

"I will put my Spirit in you and move you to follow my decrees and be careful to keep my laws" (36:27).

New Life for Dry Bones?

So remarkable is this idea that it seems Ezekiel needed to have it confirmed in a special way. It was six or seven years since he had stood in that lonely valley of the River Kebar and seen his extraordinary vision of the glory of God at the beginning of his prophetic ministry. His later ministry seems to have been characterized by far fewer visual experiences; in later chapters he speaks instead of the word of the Lord coming to him. But now at this crucial point Ezekiel's message is once again informed by the valley of vision. This time it is a vision not of divine glory but of Israel's shattered pride.

> The hand of the LORD was upon me, and he brought me out by the Spirit of the LORD and set me in the middle of a valley; it was full of bones. He led me back and forth among them, and I saw a great many bones on the floor of the valley, bones that were very dry. (37:1-2)

It is to a place of death and decay that God directs the prophet in this bizarre experience, and it is not even a cemetery with peaceful flower beds and tended gravestones. It is in fact a harrowing place of slaughter, where an ancient army had been slain in battle and the corpses left callously to rot in the open field. All that is left of them for Ezekiel to see is their skeletal remains scattered on the valley floor.

For anybody in that Middle Eastern culture, and especially for a Jew, such a site would have been full of superstitious dread and ritual defilement. Yet God seems almost to force the prophet into close contact with its gruesome desolation and its tragic despair: "He led me back and forth among them."

Why did God take Ezekiel to such a place? The clue is in 37:11: "Son of man, these bones are the whole house of Israel. They say, 'Our bones are dried up and our hope is gone; we are cut off.'"

At long last their hope was gone! The false prophets had filled them with dreams, dreams that had now been shown up as illusions, just as the dreams of Plato and More and Marx have been, and as eventually the dreams of New Age will be.

Here were the people of God, apostate, idolatrous and rebellious, and in exile they had paid the price for their sin. Now with the fall of Jerusalem, all hope of recovery had been extinguished. They were on the verge of national obliteration; they were nothing more than a pile of bones, a cemetery of memories with no future. That is the point. Bones have no future. The nation was already thoroughly corrupted by pagan religion, and now they were surrounded by the godless culture of their imperial masters. Their leadership had been deposed; their temple lay in ruins. What possible chance was there that they could ever discover the necessary strength of character to stand against this hostile environment as witnesses to the true God and his salvation? It would take a miracle, and a miracle is what happened to the dry bones.

> This is what the Sovereign LORD says: O my people, I am going to open your graves and bring you up from them; I will bring you back to the land of Israel. Then you, my people, will know that I am the LORD, when I open your graves and bring you up from them. I will put my Spirit in you and you will live, and I will settle you in your own land. Then you will know that I the LORD have spoken, and I have done it, declares the LORD. (37:12-14)

We too must sometimes tremble at the titanic opposition that the people of God face in our world today. As well as formidable areas of resistance to the gospel, and the militant anti-Christian ideologies of Islam and communism, there are the subtle pressures arising from the world that blur the distinctiveness of Christian lifestyle and conform the church to the materialistic pattern of things around it. Weakening heresies sap the spiritual vitality of God's people by casting doubt on the very Word of God. Already we see the church compromised and syncretized and apostatized in a hundred ways, its young people, children of Christian parents, growing up often godless and arrogant. We talk proudly of the Christian tradition of our culture, but there is a quiet desperation in our voice, for we know that that heritage could be irreparably lost in a single generation. The signs are that that generation is ours.

Like Israel, then, we need more than hope for the distant future. If that were all we had, we could still be thoroughly morbid and pessimistic about our environment, thinking there is nothing that can be done and that the world is just a bad, sad place that cannot be cured, only endured. With that mentality we would shrink back into our little Christian ghettos in order to survive. We would have no ambition to engage with the world and convert it. That is why we need hope for the immediate situation as well as for the long term.

Like Israel, we need to regain our confidence in the power of God to revive his people, even if the return of Christ is still many centuries away (which it may be). We need to believe that revival is possible in our day and that our energies are not wasted in praying for it and working for it. That is exactly what this vision communicates to Ezekiel: hope is not completely gone. Ezekiel is directed in his vision to two agents of revival: the Word and the Spirit.

The Word of God

> Prophesy to these bones and say to them, "Dry bones, hear the word of the LORD!" (37:4)

Some people feel that nothing can be done about the state of the church unless God takes some sovereign hand in revival. We must simply wait in Jerusalem until power falls from on high. I do not think that that is the model Jesus would have us adopt. "I tell you," says Jesus, "open your eyes and look at the fields! They are ripe for harvest" (Jn 4:35). It is never right to sit back passively and wait for revival to happen. God gives us work to do, just as he did Ezekiel.

Speaking to dry bones was, of course, a particularly ridiculous thing for God to require. Dead bones are just about the deafest thing it is possible to imagine. What on earth is the point of addressing dead bones? Apathy is probably the most demoralizing response to those who seek revival in the church. Hostility is easier to cope with than indifference. And Ezekiel's hearers were not just apathetic, they were dead; and not just dead, but decomposed! Yet God commands, "Preach to them."

Why? Because Ezekiel needed to know what every preacher, every missionary, every evangelist, every Christian needs to know as hope falls apart for the people of God: there is no situation so hopeless that the Word of God cannot evoke a response from it. It is the Word of *God*. He can bring even dry bones to life. So preach to them.

It seems stupid to proclaim God's Word to people who, humanly speaking, are incapable of either understanding or responding to our message because they are dead in trespasses and sins. But if we are going to see new life, it is through that proclaimed Word that it will come. If we are going to see revival, it will be through preaching and teaching. If revival is to come to this valley of dry bones that surrounds us, it will be led by preachers and teachers of God's Word. That is what has happened in the past: it has always been preachers who are the key to revival.

Notice two characteristics of this proclaimed Word through which the new life comes. First, its authority: "Hear the word of the LORD." That phrase occurs repeatedly in Ezekiel. It is the word of the Lord he is commanded to proclaim, not human speculation. Only the word of the Lord can bring dry bones to life. It is the word of the Lord that has the power to change. That is the only word that has any relevance to revival. Our task is to proclaim Jesus: the Jesus of the Bible, not the Jesus of human speculation or a Jesus supposedly made more credible and palatable to postmodern people. Our authority is derived only from the Bible. Only with that authority can any of us—preachers, teachers, evangelists, Christians witnessing to friends and neighbors—say, "Dry bones, hear and live!"

The second characteristic of God's Word is rather less expected: its inadequacy.

> So I prophesied as I was commanded. And as I was prophesying, there was a noise, a rattling sound, and the bones came together, bone to bone. I looked, and tendons and flesh appeared on them and skin covered them, but there was no breath in them. (37:7-8)

Ezekiel had been a prophet for many years. He had spent a long time declaring the word of the Lord to the dry bones of Israel. But up to this point, his ministry had achieved very little. The Babylonian exile had had a chastening effect on some of the people, turning them, maybe, from the idolatry that had characterized them before the conquest. Yet they were still at heart the same morally corrupt people that all human beings have always been, and the proclamation of God's Word alone could not change that. His ministry might succeed in producing a reform movement among the Jews, an initiative of moral rearmament perhaps, but it could not, in and of itself, achieve the miracle of national resurrection through the personal regeneration of the heart that Ezekiel knew was essential.

All the preaching, teaching and evangelizing in the world does not, in and of itself, have the power to revive. It may move people to a better pattern of behavior, just as the bones on the valley floor were transformed by Ezekiel's prophecy from dismembered skeletons into whole human bodies. But there was no breath in them. Proclaiming the Word cannot impart life by itself. We all know Christians and churches who in their zeal to remain faithful to the Word of God have succumbed to a dead orthodoxy. They obey the Bible very correctly, but there is no breath in them. They are morally disciplined, biblically organized and theologically reformed—but dead. The Word of God is vital in bringing life and revival to the people of God. But it is not the only thing needed.

The Spirit of God

"Prophesy to the breath; prophesy, son of man, and say to it, 'This is what the Sovereign LORD says: Come from the four winds, O breath, and breathe into these slain, that they may live.' " So I prophesied as he commanded me, and breath entered them; they came to life and stood up on their feet—a vast army. (37:9-10)

There is a double meaning in the Hebrew original of this passage which does not come through in our English translations. In the Hebrew, the word *rûaḥ* means both *breath* and *spirit*. The text is exploiting that ambiguity in the picture Ezekiel is being shown here. It graphically portrays God enlivening the external proclamation of the word with the internal quickening of his Spirit. It is this combination that brings regeneration to the human soul and revival to a people. The Word and the Spirit go together. Ezekiel sees that. Without the dynamic energy of the breath of God, his words, inspired though they are, remain sterile and fruitless. His message may achieve a measure of good, but it cannot bring about that revolution of spiritual life that is necessary if we are to be delivered from sin and discover the fullness of God's blessing.

In this Ezekiel anticipates the New Testament. Paul, as a Pharisee, learned that self-reform according to the law, while highly laudable, is not enough. We human beings are too corrupt in our hearts to become the sort of people we ought to be simply by reforming ourselves. The law is powerless, Paul says, because it is weakened by our sinful nature. It is only the Spirit of the risen Jesus, the Spirit of life, who can work the necessary miracle (see Rom 7:14—8:4).

How then are we to lay hold on this vital Spirit without whom our proclamation must be futile? The answer is implicit in the passage. "He said to me, 'Prophesy to the breath'" (37:9). Ezekiel is told to invite the Holy Spirit to perform this life-giving work that God had promised when he said that he would put his Spirit in the heart of his people (37:14). This gives us a fascinating example of the role of prayer in revival.

Prayer and proclamation cannot be separated if we want to see hope restored to the people of God in a pagan society where all hope seems gone. These are the two activities to which we must give ourselves.

Our prayers are sometimes hindered, I think, by our doubts over what difference prayer will make. That has sometimes been my problem. I remember a conversation with a Turkish friend, a Muslim, who was very dubious about the effectiveness of prayer. His comment went something like this: What is the point of praying, given that God has his plan? It's going to happen, and nothing you or I say can change it. Why, if God were to answer our prayers it would be tantamount to confessing that we know what's best for his world better than he does. No, true piety isn't to pray for things to change. It's to resign yourself to things as they are. I call it kismet, you call it predestination: the will of Allah or the will of God. What does it matter what you call it? Prayer as worship makes sense. Prayer as thanksgiving is fine. But prayers of supplication, prayers of petition, are theologically unsound. Can I suggest to God how he should run his universe?

My Muslim friend's point is worth thinking about. After all, Isaiah throws out a similar challenge: "Who . . . instructed [the LORD] as his counselor? Whom did the LORD consult to enlighten him, and who taught him the right way?" (Is 40:13). Can anyone tell the Lord what to do? Who can give him advice? Sometimes our prayers come perilously close to giving God advice. C. S. Lewis gently mocks the person whose prayer for the sick amounted to a diagnosis and a recommended prescription for treatment. In less overt ways we all pray like that.

A cross-channel ferry was having a bumpy ride. An elderly lady whose stomach was heaving with the boat spied a clergyman with a prayerbook open in his hand. "Vicar," she cried, "can't you do something about this dreadful weather?"

"Madam," he replied, "I'm in sales, not management."

Wasn't the clergyman right to suggest that his prayers would not affect the course of events? The most spiritual prayer, surely, is a prayer of resignation, not a prayer of expectation: a prayer that accepts things as they are rather than seeking to change them.

The Bible does not see it that way. In spite of its strong, lofty doctrine of the sovereignty of God, it insists that petitionary prayer works. As James says, it is "powerful and effective" (Jas 5:16). When Moses spent forty days interceding for Israel, things went differently because he had prayed. We are even told that God relented and did not do as he had threatened (Ex 32:9-14; Deut 9:13-21). What extraordinary words to use of the God of the Bible, that he should change his mind, relent! But that is not all.

The Bible frequently encourages the even greater apparent absurdity in prayer of reminding God of what he has already said. As if he could forget! By any rational argument, all such prayer must surely be at best redundant and at worst impertinent. But the Bible does not see it so. Why not? Why is Ezekiel told that he must prophesy to the breath?

My Muslim friend was right of course to believe that the world is under the control of a personal God. But he had failed to realize the means God has chosen to work out his sovereign will in the world. For extraordinary as it may seem (and it constantly amazes me), the Bible insists that the sovereign Ruler of this universe is determined to work out his purposes with our participation, our conscious and intelligent cooperation. He demands that we should not be mere pawns in his cosmic chess game; he wants us in on it. Our involvement by prayer is one of the cardinal ways in which he fulfills that intention.

That is surely why Jesus began his model prayer with "Our Father . . . " The goal of prayer is relational; it is an act of fellowship between human beings and God. Jesus repeatedly sets our understanding of intercession in the context of God's fatherly relationship with us. "Which of you fathers," he asks, "if your son asks for a fish, will give him a snake instead? . . . How much more will your Father in heaven give the Holy Spirit to those who ask him!" (Lk 11:11-13). To erect logical stumbling blocks, such as "Doesn't God already know this is what I need?" and "Who am I to tell him what to do?" is to fail to understand that we pray to a heavenly Father, not a remote tyrant and still less a mechanical blessing-dispenser. God wants to be asked. He wants to use his gifts and his blessings to develop his relationship with his people. Just as a human parent will sometimes withhold a gift until the child says "please"—because the gift will develop and express love only when it is not taken for granted or regarded as automatic—so God waits till we pray. His gifts can become vehicles of real interpersonal intimacy and communication only when we ask for them and receive them in response.

God in his grace, then, seems to have ordered his universe in such a way that his plans are often fulfilled in response to our prayers. The restoration of the nation in their land is a classic example of that. How was it that the Jews came back from exile? Without this short-term hope they would have despaired and died, whatever long-term dreams of the kingdom of God Daniel may have consoled them with. How was it fulfilled? Here is the clue:

> This is what the Sovereign LORD says: Once again I will yield to the plea of the house of Israel and do this for them: I will make their people as numerous as sheep. . . . So will the ruined cities be filled with flocks of people. (36:37-38)

There was a time when God said that he would *not* yield to the plea of the house of Israel to do anything for them. Even Noah,

Daniel and Job would not have been able to save the country by their prayers (14:12-14). Prayer had no power to reverse God's decree of judgment. Prayer is not, then, an infallible means of getting anything we want. It is not a magic spell by which we can manipulate heavenly powers to do our will. As Luther put it, "Prayer is not overcoming God's reluctance; it is laying hold of his willingness." Prayer can achieve only those outcomes that God is already waiting to bring about. It is a means of obtaining that which God has already declared he is willing to give; it is about claiming his promises.

So Ezekiel is commanded to prophesy to the breath. God requires him to pray for the nation's restoration. God is not going to do it automatically. He promised that seventy years would be the limit of their exile, but there must still be a Daniel who discovers that promise in the book of Jeremiah and bends his knee to pray for its fulfillment, and an Ezekiel who cries to the Holy Spirit to do his unique regenerative work in these dead bones. We must cry to the Holy Spirit to do that same regenerative work in dead hearts today. God waits upon the prayers of his people.

> So I prophesied as he commanded me, and breath entered them; they came to life and stood up on their feet—a vast army. (37:10)

This prophecy is fulfilled in several ways. Most immediately, it applied to the return of the Jews from exile. A purified people, faithful to God's law, returned to rebuild the city of Jerusalem in response to the prayers of Daniel, Ezra, Nehemiah and their like. God's purpose of restoration for the exiles was fulfilled.

But the prophecy was fulfilled in another sense in the birth of the church at Pentecost, when the promise came true in a new way. The Spirit of God became an indwelling presence in the heart of every individual believer. The messianic kingdom, with Jesus as the heir of David's throne, became a reality. This too came about through prayer. The believers in the upper room "all joined together constantly in prayer" (Acts 1:14).

Ezekiel's prophecy has been fulfilled as well in countless spiritual revivals down through history as this paradigm has been followed. A crippled and apostate Christianity has been stirred to life again by some new Ezekiel called Whitefield, or Wesley, or Edwards, and prayer has always been a vital component in energizing the Word of God at these times.

The day will come when this prophecy will be supremely fulfilled with the advent of a new heaven and a new earth, populated by a transformed church that will rise from the dead, not just internally through the regenerative work of the Holy Spirit but physically in new bodies. This too will be in response to his people's prayers: "Amen. Come, Lord Jesus" (Rev 22:20).

If we want to see God's purposes fulfilled, then, we must both proclaim and pray. These are the indispensable ingredients of revival. We must tell people, with the authority of God's Word, that they must repent and believe the gospel. But we must also cry to the Holy Spirit to do his indispensable and unique work of regenerating dead hearts so they may repent and believe.

There are many gimmicks assaulting the church today. There are many who hold that revival is around the corner if only we do things their way. We need to rediscover our confidence in the biblical paradigm for revival, which is always the same: proclaim and pray. Prophesy to the bones and prophesy to the Spirit.

Yet even this is not a formula (among other formulas) to guarantee that the church will grow and prosper and that Christendom will survive. " 'Proclaim and pray.' Ah! We'll organize more training for preachers and evangelists, and we'll schedule more prayer meetings. Then we'll have revival!" No; there is a third factor in this vision of dry bones, which torpedoes that kind of human self-confidence.

The Prerogative of God

He asked me, "Son of man, can these bones live?"

I said, "O Sovereign LORD, you alone know." (37:3)

There are plenty of recipes for revival and evangelistic success around today. Some preach a technique: "Follow this method and watch your church multiply." Others tell us that ecumenical cooperation is the key. Others drown us in sociological analysis: "You must understand the social mechanisms of church growth. Your evangelistic strategy must be to penetrate the homogeneous groups in your area." Still others tell us that signs and wonders will convince people of God's power and draw them into the church.

Of course there is an element of truth in all these theories. That is part of the problem with the church today! We are besieged by pressure groups, each pushing its own legitimate emphasis as if it were the sure-fire way to see the tide turned for Christendom in the West. "Do it this way!" "No, do it that way!" The average minister spins in bedazzled confusion at the statistics and the arguments that the evangelistic experts heap on his desk.

The fact is that while all these theories have value, none of them is adequate to bring about revival. The reason is that revival is always God's prerogative. "Can these bones live?" we are asked. What is the right answer to that? "Yes, if we perfect our technique of personal witness to skeletons"? "Yes, if these skeletons perceive our oneness in the Lord"? "Yes, if we penetrate the homogeneous group of skeletal society"? "Yes, if we heal a few cases of osteoarthritis in the cemetery precincts"?

The right answer is always "O Sovereign Lord, you alone know." Christian prayer is always a humble submission to the wisdom and the purpose of God: "Your kingdom come, your will be done." There were occasions when the Spirit forbade the apostle Paul to evangelize in places where God had shut the door. There have been times when he has shut the door on whole Christian churches and removed their lampstands (cf. Rev 2:5). Revival is always God's prerogative because revival always involves a miracle.

The Bible does not say that human beings are by nature spiritually weak; it says they are spiritually dead, and God alone has resurrection at his disposal. Techniques are all very well, but all the methodology in the world cannot impart the Spirit of life. Unity is important, but eleven corpses in the same coffin do not make a football team. Sociology is illuminating, but science can no more unravel the secret of revival than it can explain the empty tomb. The charismatic revolution is a fascinating phenomenon of twentieth-century church history, but no amount of witnessing signs and wonders can guarantee the experience of that greatest miracle of all, spiritual life in the heart.

We would love to believe that revival is something we can organize. But revival is something only God can do. The Spirit of God, says Jesus, cannot be organized. He is like the wind. We see the effects of his passing by, but we can never work out the laws of his operation. We can never analyze why he worked in such-and-such a place in the past, nor can we ever predict where he will work in the future. He blows where he wills (cf. Jn 3:8).

Can the Western church be delivered from its creeping paralysis, from the seeping paganism that afflicts it? Can these dry bones live? Our answer has to be "O Sovereign Lord, you alone know." Revival is possible, and we must proclaim and pray, for there is always the hope that God will again revive his people. It is equally possible that revival will not happen and that we will witness the decline of Western Christendom into a minority group in a neopagan society. It is possible that New Age mysticism will be the dominant religion of the twenty-first century and that we Christians will be fighting a rear-guard action, not unlike the Christians of the first century. Either of those possibilities could be true.

We must therefore avoid the trap of thinking that we can issue orders to the Holy Spirit or that we can manipulate him by our prayer marches or big conventions or bold prophecies, as if revival were something that we could whip up. He may use our techniques, emphases or theories. He does not have to. He does not need our officious collaboration or our expert opinion or the channels we are so diligently digging for him to flow through. In his grace he may use them, for God in his grace is often willing, even anxious, to involve us in his purposes, but not if his glory gets stolen in the process—not if we finish up putting ourselves on the pedestal, patting ourselves on the back and saying, "Didn't we do well?" Revival is a miracle of divine grace, an injection of divine power and an expression of divine sovereignty.

So proclaim the Word, in whatever sphere God has placed you. Do not be tempted to substitute anything else, no matter how relevant or appealing it may seem to turn-of-the-century people. And pray fervently, for in the economy of God, the Holy Spirit must be personally sought by God's people. He does his work of reviving individuals and groups in response to prayer. But remember that only God can give the revival we long for. So we must wait humbly. Though he delights to use us as vehicles of his Word and of his Spirit, he will not have us congratulating ourselves. When and if revival comes, he will make sure he gets the glory for it. He is the only life-giver in the universe.

> Then you will know that I the LORD have spoken,
> and I have done it. (37:14)